# Life Reimagined

# Life Reimagined

## Retirement as a Spiritual Journey

*Marilyn Sewell*

BLOOMSBURY ACADEMIC
NEW YORK • LONDON • OXFORD • NEW DELHI • SYDNEY

BLOOMSBURY ACADEMIC
Bloomsbury Publishing Inc
1359 Broadway, New York, NY 10018, USA
50 Bedford Square, London, WC1B 3DP, UK
29 Earlsfort Terrace, Dublin 2, Ireland

BLOOMSBURY, BLOOMSBURY ACADEMIC and the Diana logo are trademarks
of Bloomsbury Publishing Plc

First published in the United States of America 2026

Copyright © Bloomsbury Publishing, Inc, 2026

For legal purposes the Acknowledgments on p. vii constitute an extension of this copyright page.

Cover design: Diana Nuhn
Cover image © iStock.com / Andrii Shelenkov

All rights reserved. No part of this publication may be reproduced or transmitted in any form or by any means, electronic or mechanical, including photocopying, recording, or any information storage or retrieval system, without prior permission in writing from the publishers.

Bloomsbury Publishing Inc does not have any control over, or responsibility for, any third-party websites referred to or in this book. All internet addresses given in this book were correct at the time of going to press. The author and publisher regret any inconvenience caused if addresses have changed or sites have ceased to exist, but can accept no responsibility for any such changes.

Scriptures taken from the Holy Bible, New International Version®, NIV®. Copyright © 1973, 1978, 1984, 2011 by Biblica, Inc.™ Used by permission of Zondervan. All rights reserved worldwide. www.zondervan.com The "NIV" and "New International Version" are trademarks registered in the United States Patent and Trademark Office by Biblica, Inc.™

Library of Congress Cataloging-in-Publication Data Available

ISBN: HB: 979-8-7651-5784-8
PB: 979-8-7651-5783-1
ePDF: 979-8-7651-5787-9
eBook: 979-8-7651-5785-5

Typeset by Deanta Global Publishing Services, Chennai, India
Printed and bound in the United States of America

To find out more about our authors and books visit www.bloomsbury.com
and sign up for our newsletters.

*For my sons, Kash and Madison*

# Contents

*Prologue* x

## I   Arriving  1

1  Clearing Out  3
2  What's It All About, Alfie?  7
3  Leaving Church  13
4  Breaking Free  19
5  Surrender  23
6  Starr King  27
7  Searching  31
8  Finding  35
9  Coming into My Own  39

## II   Falling  43

10  Losing  45
11  Growing-Up Days  49
12  Grieving  53
13  Looking for Home  57
14  Surprised by Joy  61
15  Too Much, Too Soon  65
16  My Body, My Self  69
17  Falling into Despair  73

## III  Searching  77

**18**  Looking for Answers  79
**19**  Involuntary Job Loss  83
**20**  Males Are More Vulnerable  85
**21**  Some Age Out  89
**22**  Some Continue to Work  93
**23**  Work Ethic in My Family  97
**24**  Taking Care of Business  103
**25**  Who Are My People Now?  107
**26**  Letting Go  113
**27**  Creating a New Narrative  117

## IV  Reflecting  125

**28**  The More That Haunts Our Days  127
**29**  Dreams Change  131
**30**  What Must I Do to Be Saved?  135
**31**  Where Does the Light Lead?  139
**32**  When Less Becomes More  143
**33**  The Season of Loss  147
**34**  What Gifts Are Ours to Give?  151
**35**  Bestowing a Blessing  155

## V  Becoming  161

**36**  A Great Cloud of Witnesses  163
**37**  Do the Right Thing  167
**38**  Continuing to Minister  173
**39**  Ministry of the Word  179
**40**  A Journal of the Plague Years  183
**41**  What Goes, What Stays  189
**42**  Living in Love  193

**43** Choosing Mercy over Judgment 199
**44** The Scream of a Whistle 203
**45** Nothing, No Matter How Precious, Can Be Kept 209
**46** The Order of Things 213

*About the Author* 217

# Prologue

*There is no object that we see, no action that we do, no good that we enjoy, no evil that we feel or fear, but we may make some spiritual advantage of. And he that makes such improvement is wise as well as pious.*

"For My Dear Son," by Anne Bradstreet, 1630

A venerable institution founded in 1866, the First Unitarian Church of Portland, Oregon, had never had a female minister—until I arrived in 1992. This church was precisely the place I'd been led by my whole life and experience. I loved ministry, and I stayed at the church for seventeen years. Parts of the job were wrenchingly hard, but I saw my work as a spiritual calling, one that brought all my past experience together, allowing me to use myself well in the world.

As a single woman, I had hoped a partner would appear when I settled down in Portland. Looking back, I should not have been surprised that no romantic relationship worked: I was married to the church. It was a trade-off that women in demanding careers have historically made, and I don't regret a day of it. I gave myself to a holy union that made me feel loved, helped me grow, and, most importantly, grounded me in purposes larger than myself.

But every good thing must come to an end, of course, and my age and the evolving needs of the church told me it was time to retire. Sensing I was in dangerous territory, I did all the right things: I read, consulted, considered, planned. But no consultant, no book, no friend could have prepared me for the emptiness, the lack of purpose, the loss of my community I experienced. I had been the captain of a grand ship, and then my ship sailed on without me, leaving me standing on the shore, bereft.

I wondered if I could ever again feel that I had "come round right," as I had at the church. My spiritual dilemma became: *am I "done" now? If not, what is my new call?* Unmoored, with a deep sense of loss and crippling anxiety, I was pushed to go deeper than I yet had gone, deeper than I wanted to go, to get at the roots of my despair.

I found myself awash in profound questions of being: "Who am I, without my identity as the minister of First Unitarian? What, if anything, could life possibly hold for me now? How could I find a sustaining community? What do I need to let go of, as not being worthy of the time I have left? What will my legacy be?" I searched and searched for signs, solutions.

When I started writing this book, I thought it might give direction and comfort to others. That was the minister speaking. I was seven years wandering through the thicket before I felt I could even begin to give voice to the challenges I faced. And it has taken four more years to complete the book. As it turned out, I found I was writing *Retirement as a Spiritual Journey* for myself, and as I wrote, the book was teaching me both how to write it and how to grow into the next stage of my life. Some painful truths presented themselves, surprising me, and the process yielded contradictions as well as conclusions.

I'm not quite the same person now as when I started this book. And that's all to the good. My struggles were not unique—so perhaps you will see yourself in these pages. If my book has any value, it will be because it confirms our mutual quest for joy and meaning, at whatever age. What else are we to be about but this?

# I
# Arriving

# 1

## *Clearing Out*

It's spring. I'm sorting out my closet, getting rid of clothes I no longer wear. I'm stacking them in three different piles: Goodwill, Dress for Success, and Eileen Fisher Green. Goodwill gets T-shirts and guilt-producing jeans that are too small. After about ten years or so of denial, of fantasizing about myself in my thin-people clothes and feeling sure I will lose ten pounds soon, I have now admitted that I will never again be a size 12. Not going to happen. Cambio has to go, as well as Not Your Daughter's Jeans, two sizes too small.

As I work at this task of relinquishment, I still cling to certain special items from my youth. Like that fine old rust-colored leather tote that I bought in Italy, maybe forty years ago. Buffed up, it looks great, better than ever, I thought—the scratches and worn areas make it that much more handsome. But now I'm seeing its scars with new eyes: the leather cord around the bottom is loose and can't be replaced. The stitching in the straps is weakening, breaking in various places. *But wait! The leather is still gorgeous. I can't just throw it out.* No, I decide. It's beyond repair. Done, finished. I toss it.

I find the long cotton dress, bone, with peach embroidery on the bodice—I hold it up, and remember. Back in the 1970s the dress made me feel "like an actual woman," as the song goes. I run my fingers over the stitches, lovingly made by some woman so many years ago. There's the floral nightgown and robe set from Neiman Marcus, a luxury I would never have allowed myself, given to me by my fiancé's mother the Christmas I became engaged to her son; the sexy red halter top with white polka dots; the cream jersey blouse with the sparkle at the deep neckline—too splashy, but I love its verve. The clothing brings back times of pleasure and passion, *oh, that night at the pig roast!* All the promises of youth that are too soon dashed by age and circumstance. As I touch each of these garments, I say to myself, *one day I will want to wear that!* But then I admit those days are gone, never to return. It's the memories I can't stand to let go of.

Here's the power dress, navy blue with the large shoulder pads, the one I wore to City Club before I figured out that not much of consequence happens there. Here's the long black tunic top, matching mid-length black skirt, the sleek outfit I used for public speaking. And there's the striking off-white suit with fringe on the jacket from St. John for more formal occasions. Bought on sale, but still way too expensive: a parish minister needs to model conservative dress and good taste more than humility. At least in my downtown church in Portland, Oregon.

The shoulders of these garments are collecting dust. *Still, I might need them someday, you never know . . .* I'm clinging to the remnants of my former life. The life so full of purpose and possibility. Keeping my professional garb has allowed me to believe that nothing has really changed, has subverted my rising consciousness that I'm on track to the end of things—*not just of career, but of life itself.*

・・・・・・

When I first arrived in Portland to begin my ministry, I had to clothe myself. Literally. For years during graduate school, I had worn the same beige corduroy pants and matching jacket—a cozy and reliable outfit. I didn't care to be fashionable; I wasn't dressing to impress anyone or to attract attention to my body—I was well into the life of the mind, doing my dissertation: my days were filled with reading, thinking, writing. I did not wear a bra—this was Berkeley, after all, and comfort was my concern. Also, money was tight—so tight I had to consider whether or not to buy a cup of coffee at Peet's on any given day.

Upon arriving in Portland, I went to Nordstrom and asked for help. A personal dresser, Mary, came to my rescue. Used to dressing stylish women with money, Mary was taken aback when I undressed in the fitting room. Always tactful with her recommendations, she simply said, "I think we should start with underwear." Onward, then, to respectability.

I wore only suits and high heels for the first six or eight years of my ministry, partly to win the approval of the older, wealthier members, who had wanted yet another male minister and were reluctant to accept a woman—in particular, one with a Southern accent. Later, foot problems took me to Birkenstocks, so I chose midi-skirts and handwoven shawls, which I wore well with my tall figure. I never dressed like my staff, who tended toward relaxed, informal clothing; nor would I dress like my congregants—unlike attendees in mainline churches, these doubters and skeptics were not fearful enough of God to dress up for the worship service. I was never carelessly dressed, never sexy—certainly never a hint of cleavage—I went for quiet elegance and modesty. Even in the grocery store. A minister is a minister wherever they go. They will be judged as an emissary, I knew, so I tried not to let my appearance mess with anybody's ideas of God. God is not sexy or fashionable. Or poor.

Such a simple task, cleaning out the closet. Giving away clothing I haven't used . . . for seven years. It took me a long time to get here. As I discard my clothing, I am discarding my identity as well. I keep only the informal attire, the pants and tops. They hang there, a bit forlorn in the half-empty closet. I'm making space for the new life I'm creating.

*I meet a friend for tea. She wants to check out the dress shop across the road. I love design, love fabric, so sure, I'll go. I admire a blouse, try it on. It suits me exactly: a good grade of cotton, tucks at the shoulder, falling full below, small brown wooden buttons. My friend says, Wow! The shop clerk says, Perfect! But I demur, making some lame excuse. The real reason I don't buy it is that I don't need it. I have more clothes now than I have places to wear them.*

# 2

# *What's It All About, Alfie?*

I watch Frank Capra's film *It's a Wonderful Life* every Christmas. Lots of people do. And why? We see George Bailey in despair, thinking of suicide, then we watch the angel Clarence help him understand what his hometown would have been like had he never existed. We want confirmation that our living—in spite of our mistakes, misjudgments, lapses of virtue—has made a difference for others, as indeed it has, though not only in entirely positive ways.

What gives our life meaning? What is the purpose of my existence, anyway? Most of us don't ask these formidable questions during our younger years, when the tasks of life are clear and immediate: *graduate, find a job, find a mate, find a better job, buy a house, maybe have a child or two*. We don't have time to delve into "the meaning of life"—it's enough to try to meet the demands of the day. But when we retire . . . well, that clear line of progress gets fuzzy. Are we supposed to relax, have some fun, and then die? What's the game plan? There's no clear, easy answer.

All human giving is creative and nurturing in that it supports life and counters death. What we offer to others is reciprocal, for we both give what we most desire—the promise of new life—and receive the same, ever more richly. It really is, quite literally, more blessed to give than to receive. So how do we maintain that vital connection, that give and take with others, if our chief means of giving is our job, now that our job is gone?

I've always seen pregnant women as holy vessels of life, inspiring wonder and awe. For me, giving birth was the clearest, most obvious act of giving. When my body was swelling with a developing child, I had no concerns, no questions about meaning or purpose. My body, my whole being, was given over to the new life within. I had to take care of myself—I felt I was partaking in the most sacred act of existence.

There are other circumstances in which questions about meaning give way to the demands of the moment. Consider the soldier on patrol in enemy territory, keenly alive and awake, as in no other place, no other time. He is protecting his own life and the lives of his fellow soldiers. He might even sacrifice his own life to save another. He must put aside his grief as he sees his brothers die. Meaning is not elusive, it is omnipresent. As one vet put it, "I hated my deployment, but I also knew every minute of every day why I was there and what I was supposed to do." This experience of intense presence often makes a return to civilian life difficult. Longing for the clarity of battle, when questions about meaning were put to rest, the veteran may find other pursuits shallow, superficial. Family and friends may not understand his lassitude, may be surprised that he wants to volunteer for another stint in the battlefield, where his life may in fact be lost.

All of us may, to some degree, share this loss of meaning when our particular ways of giving are done. Certain questions surprise us with their power and immediacy.

Consider the following scenario: in your youth, you have a sense of potency, an organic response to the call of life itself. Your future invites possibility, gives way to the next phase and the next and the next, always moving you along to a new place. Through the years, you gain knowledge, know-how, confidence. You have times of unhappiness, setbacks, maybe even times of despair—but that state can change, and almost always does.

You are ever rising to your unique beauty, your power of person—you can initiate, perhaps move others to task; you can choose a worthy goal, move toward it, watch it bear fruit. Your sense of agency draws you on. You are attentive to fresh opportunities. Unless inhibited by illness of mind or body, or by constraining circumstances—or even in spite of these difficulties—you gather with others to shape and sustain life. You become a teacher, a shopkeeper, a driver, a salesperson, a baseball player, a doctor, a farmer, a roustabout, a musician. You do your part. You *work*.

You hardly notice, though, how your options narrow as the years pass, and since you don't really feel your age, you think you can always take that biking trip to the south of France, come upon a new love, or move to a more interesting job. Then some surprise occurs: *the medical tests show . . . the accident happens . . . the vows are broken . . .* , and a new consciousness wakes you from the fantasy that you will live forever, that aging is for others. You find that you cannot endlessly explore new paths of work or relationship. You've made choices, and these choices bring limits you hadn't recognized: you come to understand the profound truth of the old maxim, *one thing leads to another*.

You turn fifty, whoa, that's a big one! Then, a few short years later, sixty, then almost overnight, sixty-five. *Could it already be time to retire?* You may leave on a high note, celebrated—or face an unexpected loss when your company downsizes. But even for those who don't particularly identify with their job, retirement is the end of the party. You move out of the community of those whose work maintains and transforms the world. You are no longer a player—you do not roll the dice, you are not in the game. You do not hitch the horse, saw the board, create the path through the wilderness. With this falling away of role, you are surprised and confounded by your vulnerability.

The retiree becomes, from this perspective, irrelevant. *Of course, I'm relevant! I'm precisely the same person I've always been.* Yes and no. You definitely are not indispensable. In fact, the shocking news, the completely unacceptable news, is that you are entirely dispensable—whether you are a general or a house cleaner. Someone else will fill the gap as soon as you make room. Haven't you seen it happen over and over again? Your primary care doctor of many years retires, and you are bereft: *she knows me, she cares, what will I do?* But then you meet your new young doctor and find him both capable and caring. You begin to let go and reattach.

The truth is that when you retire, you've been relegated to the outside of the community, out of the circle of life—you're now one of those whose days lead inexorably to frailty, forgetfulness, and finally death. Repression is no longer an option. It has always been there—this knowledge of our mortality—but with retirement, that vague knowing becomes the gestalt that haunts our days.

We all know we are going to die—that's patently clear, as soon as Goldie goes belly up in the fishbowl and Mom explains *she is in heaven, not to worry, we can get a new one.* Not Goldie, but another fish. Our fate seems entirely understandable and acceptable, so long as it's kept at the cognitive level. But when we first internalize that knowing—take it from the abstract to the flesh, to the blood and bone and breath, whether that's at age twenty-one or fifty-eight or seventy-three—we are likely shaken to the core.

Retirement is often the first time people are led to ask questions like *What is the meaning of my life? What will my legacy be?* We understand we no longer have weeks, even hours, to squander. We are carnal; our days are as the Psalmist writes, "a shadow that passes away."

*A friend gives me an amaryllis bulb for Christmas, a Red Lion, the tag says. I water it, wait impatiently for it to wake up. Two weeks after Christmas, well into the New Year, four magnificent blooms slowly unwrap from the green. As I attempt to stake it, my plant falls to the floor, the fragile stem fractures. I am horrified. I go for the scotch tape! Foolish me. Of course, it's done. It's done.*

・・・・・・

As for me, the ways of giving that made my life meaningful were no longer there. I was a leader. Who would I lead? I was a preacher. But I no longer had a pulpit. I was full of analysis, commentary about current events, but I was no longer tapped for interviews. Pastoral care was one of the most satisfying parts of ministry—I counted it a privilege to be trusted by congregants during times of confusion and loss. Now no one was calling for appointments. I was surprised and unnerved by the fact that *nothing was required of me*. I was undone. I needed to place my offering on an altar somewhere.

My dilemma was commonplace, I was to learn. I had a happenstance meeting with the daughter of a farmer who had been struck with serious depression and had to be hospitalized. She said her father had sold his small farm and no longer had his stand at the farmer's market. His work was gone, his community was gone. He no longer had a place where he belonged, where he could give.

I'm remembering a conversation with my doctor. I'm telling her of the anguish I'm feeling since I retired, how lost and depressed I am. She glances down, pauses, then looks at me and says, "My father was a well-known lawyer, the rainmaker in a large firm. He retired and three months later, he killed himself. He said, 'What's the point?'" Yes, this is the existential question that dogs our days when we're unconnected from any larger purpose: *What's the point?* Who am I, if not a lawyer or a fisherman or a singer?

*Nanook of the North* (1922), thought to be the first documentary film ever made, is the story of an Eskimo (now known as an Inuit), one of three hundred nomadic people who live on the eastern shores of Hudson's Bay in the unforgiving cold of Canada's north. Their travel is largely through kayak in the summer and dog sled during the winter. Life is primarily one of subsistence—Nanook and the other men hunt for food to keep their families alive. In the film, we see Nanook moving through the forbidding wilderness of snow and ice. He leaves every place he touches better than when he arrived, for he knows that someone else, some lonely traveler, may pass there, and he wants to make their journey easier. It is a powerful lesson. Ultimately, this may be all we can do to counter the sheer, unmitigated loss of our own life: *make the path easier for another.*

# 3

# *Leaving Church*

I thought I was prepared for retirement.

I had been the senior minister of a large Unitarian Universalist church in Portland, Oregon, for seventeen years. It was the second Unitarian church founded on the West Coast, after San Francisco, when Portland had a population of about 5,000, and with its founding, the church began a long history of civic involvement. The first minister, the youthful Thomas Lamb Eliot, came around the Cape of Good Hope, arriving in Portland on a rainy Christmas Eve, 1867, with his wife and infant son. He was to be there for twenty-six years. He and his congregation founded almost every charitable institution in Portland, including the Humane Society, the public library, the Boys and Girls Club. The church's lecture series was the impetus for Reed College, founded in 1908.

I arrived in 1991, and the city, then over 865,000 people, had remained progressive but was also beset by a far-right movement. First Unitarian was amenable to my far-left politics and open to my message for social justice. Precisely the right setting for me. I was able to invite people into a church community where they could flourish personally and also make a difference in their city and the larger world.

All my life had prepared me for this position. I had studied broadly in literature, social work, and theology; I had worked as a writer, a counselor, and had even done a television advice show—all of this came together in my ministry. Besides which, I was able to use all the human stuff of the past fifty years: the pain and loneliness of my growing-up days, my marriage and divorce, my difficulty mothering, my spiritual searching.

Perhaps most significant for me personally, the parish gave me a way of loving. Intimacy had been difficult for me, always, and I despaired of ever finding a partner, but I could love my congregants from my lofty pulpit, without getting too close, without risking too much emotionally. I could be there at the hospital, hold a trembling hand after surgery, pray with them. I could be their strong, sure voice in a city, in a country, that was crying for justice. So many healers emerge from long-standing wounds, and I was no exception. I had found a way to love from afar.

When we find the place that "comes round right," we enter a contentment which is elusive for most people, most of the time. We are wanting creatures, and the good fortune to be so completely engaged is a little like falling in love—all seems well with your soul. Romantic love is often an illusion that does not hold, whereas doing the work you were meant to do gives a satisfaction that endures. To lose my church, then, was to lose the anchor which kept me from drifting loose, floundering in the shallows.

So why did I choose that moment in time to retire? I had no future plans. I was an introvert with little taste for social life. I was sixty-eight, but in good health. The church was humming along, people were packing the pews. On the surface of things, leaving the church did not seem like a wise move. Why would I leave a job I loved for such an ill-defined future?

The short answer is that I wanted to write something other than sermons. Preaching is not an easy task, and sermons are unlike any other artistic genre. I had been writing and speaking for years in various venues before I took a pulpit, but like most ministers, my early efforts at preaching were . . . well, mediocre. After years of learning my craft, though, I had developed the skills to construct, write, and preach a sermon. I knew how to focus my subject, how to use story and poetic expression, how to use humor for relief and emphasis. After the requisite researching and contemplation, I could turn out a sermon in anywhere from three to five hours, and I didn't think I could improve by more effort or experience. Just as I had felt drawn to Portland as a kind of inevitability, now I felt I needed to explore other kinds of creative expression.

And then a second and even more important consideration was the current state of the organization—there was literally no more room for the people who wanted to attend Sunday services. When a sanctuary becomes 80 percent filled, people begin to feel crowded and attendance will plateau—that's precisely where we were at First Unitarian. Various solutions were possible: we could add a third service, but I no longer had the stamina to preach three services. Or we could start a new church in the suburbs of Portland. Or we could build another sanctuary that would hold more worshippers. All difficult, exacting tasks.

These years had been good years—perhaps the best years of my life. Who would not want to pull together with others to right the ship of state, so stuck in the mud of human ignorance and depravity? Who wouldn't want to be a part of the rescue crew? I wanted to go on forever this way. But I couldn't. The mortal flesh fails—bones creak, eyes dim, steps falter, mind skips a beat, fatigue sets in. My body was giving me the message that maybe my giving tree was weakening at the core, the branches straining to flower. I knew I did not have the years in me to take the church to the next level. And if I wanted to make a serious effort at creative writing, the time was at hand.

・・・・・・

My decision to leave the church was a thoughtful one. I did all the right things—read, considered, meditated, prayed, planned. Determined to follow all the rules and recommended procedures, I let the board know two years ahead of time, and we retained a consultant to help us through the transition. I began slowly pulling back from my work, as he suggested, exploring other interests. I already had a second career underway as a writer, and a filmmaker had begun a feature-length documentary, *Raw Faith*, about my life and work. I had saved carefully and was untroubled by financial concerns. I had made my home in Portland, Oregon, at that time one of the most livable cities on the planet. I figured I would do retirement the way I had done everything else—astonishingly well. I was your overachiever's overachiever. Except in the art of love—love had been ever elusive for me. I had resigned myself to being alone for the rest of my life.

Even as I tried to prepare the staff for my absence, giving Tom Disrud, the associate minister, ever more responsibility, I began to somehow run into conflict. I had turned much of my focus to the documentary film, seeing that project as a gift to the larger world, but some of the staff resented the time given to the film. Tension began to rise in the ranks, no one seemed settled, secure. What had I done wrong?

I was far from faultless as a leader—I could be blunt and insensitive at times. Some humanist congregants didn't care for my theology. And a few others resented my emphasis on justice work: five families of wealth left the church during my tenure. No doubt there were those who were happy with my leave-taking, as would be true of any minister. I called my friend Linda, the director of ministry at the Unitarian Universalist Association, trying to make sense of the distress I was sensing in the system. She was not surprised. She simply said, "Breaking up is hard to do." Indeed. Perhaps for staff, some kind of betrayal, an abandonment, had taken place. Their leader was jumping ship. What would happen to them? To the church?

I found myself a stranger in a strange land. Nothing—no article, no conversation, no consultant—could have prepared me for the reality of giving over my keys to the church and walking out the door: the profound emptiness, the lack of purpose, the isolation. I never could have anticipated the sense of rejection, of no longer being needed or wanted. Dreams haunted my sleep.

*I am driving to my class to teach, but I can't find the way. The road is unfinished, no signage. I know my students are waiting. The principal will be worried—she will blame me. I panic. I pull up across the road from a large, faceless institution. I go inside the building, where I meet a series of people who seem friendly and willing to help, each gives me directions. But each time I try to find my way, I become lost again. I'm trying to get out of the building, I keep coming to blind corners, dead ends. I realize that I'm going to be very late, I call the principal on my cell phone. She is angry, she says that the children have been left alone. This is a new job, and I'm failing at it. Can't someone help me find my way? A chain-link fence surrounds the building. I search for an opening in the fence, maybe somewhere another person has broken through. Who? Who can help me?*

· · · · · ·

For seventeen years, I had invited congregants on Sunday morning into a worship service that grounded us in a set of values and traditions, giving us courage for the demands of our lives. Our voices would swell: *O God, our help in ages past, our hope for years to come.* I would bring to our common concern the injuries, the illnesses, perhaps tell of one who had died. I would step into the pulpit, each time with the same prayer on my lips: *May the words of my mouth and the meditations of my heart be acceptable in thy sight, my strength and my redeemer.* At the end of the sermon, I would take a breath, *Will you pray with me,* I would say. We had come together as one body, a sacred unity.

One day I was representing First Unitarian in the media and in the public square, giving interviews and speeches. I was marrying congregants and burying their kin. I was counseling them about the various losses humans predictably suffer: the splendid worker who got cruelly downsized; the woman whose husband has just surprised her by leaving; the man, in despair, who has just been told he has Alzheimer's. I was dedicating infants, touching their foreheads with water, giving them to the care and nurturance of the community. The next day, I was putting away my red doctoral robe, storing the leather briefcase given to me by the congregation on my tenth anniversary.

Back at home, I began rearranging my bookcase. No need for Kierkegaard, I thought, Tillich could go. I was so wrong. I needed them more than ever to ground me as I moved through my loss to some new place of understanding, some new way of placing my offerings on the altar. Always there had been a next big thing, and now there was not. Was there not to be more growing and becoming, beckoning me on? I had lost so much that had given my life meaning. I had no clarity, few patterns to guide me.

Is the next chapter only aging and death? Desperate visits to the gym to regain strength; appointments with various doctors, physical therapists; cold packs, hot packs; medication for this and that; deep breathing exercises to comfort my scared heart? Am I fated to tumble downhill at an ever-increasing rate? The culture kept flashing images before me of youth and energy, of beauty and fun. Where was my place in all that? I found myself adrift in a sea that had no demarcation point.

*I am inside the edge of a large circular crevasse, hundreds of feet down, dark. I'm hanging on by my fingers, working my way carefully around, looking for some place to hold on, to pull myself up out of danger—but I can't find anything. I thought this place was familiar, but now I can't seem to find any place to hold on. I hope someone will come to help, but no one comes.*

# 4

# *Breaking Free*

My career was never a straight line. I had been an English teacher in New Orleans, had published my first article in a national magazine in my twenties, but like many women who came of age in the 1950s, I assumed my true destiny was to find a good man and live vicariously through him.

I was teaching at Benjamin Franklin High in New Orleans, a public school for gifted students, when I met Frank at a book discussion group sponsored by a Presbyterian church less than a block from where I lived just off St. Charles Avenue. Actually, we were both looking for a partner, not really conversation about books—ironically, though, the book being discussed was Betty Friedan's *The Feminine Mystique*. The times they were a-changin'.

Frank was late for the meeting, so he missed the entire discussion, but I engaged him in conversation afterward and found he was a doctor doing a surgery residency at Charity Hospital. Bingo! As we stood in front of the church saying goodbye, he asked for my phone number. He wore pleated pants, way outdated even for that era. He was jangling, jangling, jangling the loose change in his pocket. I knew he wanted me. And I knew he would never leave me.

I loved teaching at Franklin and had run a couple of summer programs for LBJ's Great Society. I left my job. I left a cozy apartment in a Victorian house. I left my friends. My church. I got married, ordered stationery that read "Mrs. Frank Sewell, Jr." We spent our first summer at a rural hospital, where Frank assisted the only surgeon in town. The locals referred to me as "the doctor's wife." In September, we sailed on the Queen Elizabeth II to Liverpool, England, where for two years, Frank did a pediatric surgery residency. I taught English to middle school boys—a disastrous experience, for they couldn't understand my Southern accent, nor I, their Liverpudlian speech—until I gave birth to my first son. I was pregnant with my second son when we moved to my husband's home in Lexington, Kentucky. I had followed the script so very well.

But it turned out that my role in this drama—essentially a support system for a surgeon—was not amenable to the woman I was becoming. It was, in fact, making me crazy. As a young mother of two toddlers, I found myself bored and frustrated. And in therapy for depression. I would write in snatches and squirrel away the pages in a lower kitchen cabinet. I never spoke to my husband about my writing: he was a surgeon doing significant work in the world—saving people's lives, for god's sake—and I had not yet understood that words could save lives.

I decided to sign up for a writing course with Wendell Berry, a poet, novelist, and essayist who was teaching at the University of Kentucky and was just becoming well known. After all, I had been an English major. I knew how to *write*. I could garner some badly needed strokes here, I thought.

The Inuit have a word for artistic concentration: *quarrtisiluni*, which literally means "a waiting for something to break." A perfect description of my psychic condition when I walked into Wendell's class and took my seat. I was unprepared for the power of that first encounter.

Wendell read to us from *Paradise Lost*, then read a short story by his friend Gurney Norman, an initiation story set in Eastern Kentucky. I was moved by this teacher, and I didn't quite know why. His voice was soft, all Kentucky, but he spoke out of some deep place within himself, some place of integrity and purpose. When he laughed, that too came from the depths of his being. *Here is a man whose life is given over. I want to be with him for a while and learn what I can.*

For our first assignment, I wrote a long discursive essay on examinations. An arbitrary choice. I was confident that my essay was well-written—carefully reasoned, graceful, perfectly punctuated. Wendell returned our papers at the end of the next class. I could hardly believe his response—there was no grade, just a blanket rejection: "Give me something of yourself." *I had come for praise, and I got this? What could he mean?* The other students trooped out. I stood there, staring at my paper, unable to move, and cried. There's no other way to put it. I was a 34-year-old woman weeping big crocodile tears. An inauspicious beginning.

All that semester, Wendell kept sending my papers back, no comments at all. All during my academic career in college and graduate school, I was the quintessential straight-A student. All my other teachers had told me how good I was. Wendell was the only one who asked for more. And he was the only one who taught me anything about writing. "Tell the truth about what you know," he said.

But telling the truth was the most difficult thing in the world for me. I was beginning to understand what that kind of honesty means for a writer: the choice of a single word can reveal an old desperation still alive; a metaphor that takes you unaware can awaken you, can quite literally change the course of your life.

All that semester, I continued to write essays, articles, and book reviews, some published in the *Lexington Herald Leader*. I gave Wendell nothing of myself. As a matter of fact, I even reviewed his new book, *The Memory of Old Jack*, for the paper. *Ha! Take that!* But something in me was moving.

The night before the last class, I sat up till dawn writing an autobiographical essay on the old Remington Rand portable typewriter I was given by my father when I graduated from high school. I finished it with my three-year-old son Kash sitting on my lap. I'd had no sleep at all, no time to edit the piece. I got ready for class, but then a major snag—the babysitter didn't show up. *What was I to do?*

It was December, and big, soft, white flakes were wafting down. I dressed my curly headed boys in their little snow suits, secured them in the back seat of our red Volvo station wagon, and drove to Good Samaritan Hospital. The children and I rode the elevator to the fourth floor, where their father was doing surgery. I dropped them off at the nurses' station and said, "Dr. Sewell will have to take care of his sons this morning." The nurses pitched in with goodwill, and I left for class. I don't know what possessed me to do this, because I am a good girl, always have been. I just knew that at all costs, I had to be in class that day.

Wendell began the class by going around the circle and asking if anyone had a piece to read. I always sat just to his left, so he started with me. "Marilyn, would you like to read?"

"Oh, I don't know," I said, and waved him off.

So he went right round the circle, asking everyone else, but it was final exam time so he came up empty. Turning again to me, he said, "Well, let's start over. Marilyn, do you have anything you can read?"

"Yes," I said, "I guess I could read something."

And I read and read and read—nineteen pages worth. For the first time in my life, I owned the truth about myself. I told about my failure as a teacher, about my depression, my loneliness, my anger, my loving, my doubt, my joy, my fear, my lack of faith. I was crying as I read—I never once looked up from my paper. When I finished, I threw the pages at Wendell—half in spite and half in triumph—and said, "There! That's what you wanted."

It was only then that I became aware of the other students—I saw that they were crying, too. They didn't offer the usual critique. They just listened. And witnessed. Each one came in turn, gave me a hug, then left silently. Wendell had a tear edging out of his eye. He said gruffly, "Now don't let yourself think of this as finished."

No, nothing was finished—but much was just beginning. No secrets need be held. I was free. Though the leave-taking was several years in the making, when I walked out of that classroom, I knew my marriage was over.

I continued my work with Wendell, doing independent study. Once I happened upon him in front of an elevator at the university, and I said spontaneously, "Wendell, you changed my life." He would have none of it. He said, "No, I didn't change your life. You changed your life. I just asked you to use words well." It is a dangerous endeavor, using words well, as I discovered. The changes that were precipitated were not easy, not for me, not for others.

# 5

# *Surrender*

Divorce is commonplace, after all—almost 50 percent of marriages don't last. But commonplace is not the same as easy: trust me, divorce is never easy. I left a good man who loved me, lost warm relationships with his family, lost friends. I lost my church community, as well, since the Southern Baptists declared me a sinner for leaving Frank. I also took my two young boys away from their father during the week and served them up a wicked stepmother on weekends.

    I became a single mother with two toddlers and no job. *What about IBM, I thought—the company had a huge center in Lexington—surely they could use someone like me, with my MA in English, my Phi Beta Kappa distinction.* Wanting to look the part for my interview, I bought a dark suit and an expensive leather briefcase, a costume I thought would impress corporate America. I was offered a job as a secretary. *How could I be so well-educated, yet not find work?* I heard "overqualified" more than once from prospective employers.

    I decided to go for a master's in clinical social work, which I thought would allow me to make not a good living, but at least a living. My timing was abysmal: Ronald Reagan was elected president, and social workers were being laid off left and right, thus allowing the poor to pull themselves up by their nonexistent bootstraps. I lost three jobs in two years and found myself standing in unemployment lines, wondering how I would pay the mortgage for the home I got in the divorce settlement. I remember going to a financial adviser and asking for help in balancing my budget. She said, "It's not that you don't manage your money well, it's that you don't have enough money."

For seven years, I was filled with uncertainty and indecision, moving from one low-paying job to another, and caring for my sons. Despondent, I began considering some kind of further study that would yield a new career. I thought about getting a PhD in education or perhaps in social work. I traveled to Smith College to check out their social work program—I found the department surprisingly elitist, given their mission to help the poor and disadvantaged. Then I traveled to Brandeis and talked with David Gil, a teacher who had impressed me with his social analysis when I'd heard him speak in Lexington. But he told me Brandeis had gone over to the dark side in their efforts to get grants, and had he not had tenure, they would have gotten rid of him. Not an atmosphere I wanted to enter.

· · · · · ·

As a child I had been "saved" and baptized, twice actually, once by the Catholics and once by the Southern Baptists, but I had still felt I was in control of my destiny—I mean, I *had* to be, didn't I? Who else? God's role was to look on fondly and not guilt me too much since I—well, *religiously*—followed all the rules. I saw even the divorce as a Spirit-led decision, or at least an escape from a domestic role that was making me sick to death. My personal narrative—poor, unloved girl marries a doctor, has two remarkable children, and lives a respectable and affluent life—took a deep dive and was shattered to bits upon landing.

There were dangers, toils, and snares. It was the 1970s, and so there were a number of men, some overlapping, as I acted out the adolescence I had not as yet experienced. I was attractive to men because we had a lot in common: we just wanted good sex, and we definitely did not want marriage. My depression turned manic, and I spent a couple of weeks in a hospital mental ward. Then one morning, driving home from my TV advice show, one of two jobs I worked, I had a grand mal seizure at 60 miles per hour. Somehow, my ancient blue-green Olds with the big fins cruised all by itself into a service station, stopping right by the pumps. I was spared injury and woke up in an emergency vehicle calling out the names of my children. A week of medical tests in the hospital yielded a diagnosis of stress.

I was awash in unknowing, and desperate. When I thought I could go no lower, I literally and figuratively got down on my knees and asked whatever powers that be to allow me to use my life, such as it was, for the good. Similar to what happens to alcoholics and drug addicts when they lose everything and gain in return a whole shitload of humility.

That's it. Full stop. End of prayer.

I didn't know at the time that I would become a minister and a writer, but at that moment I reassessed my claim on my personal virtue and consecrated myself to . . . well, something greater than myself. I didn't know if there was a God, still don't, but I figured out that I'm not God, and that's the starting point of any spiritual journey. Abject failure and bewilderment turned into what theologians call a *kairotic moment*.

I've never escaped periods of doubt and darkness, but going forward, my only plan was to *discern and follow*, trusting that the way would be made known. In truth, I'm more of an agnostic than a believer—doubt seems to have a lot more integrity when it comes to relating to the infinite. There's a great mystery that will always be beyond me and all the genius physicists in the world. I entered the foolishness of those without hope or procedures or plans: I put all my trust in something I hardly understood. Everything went into the one flimsy valise of my faith.

By this time, I had started attending the Unitarian Universalist Fellowship in Lexington, where I found a measure of acceptance and community. I had shared my employment problems with the young minister, Roger Fritts, who told me about the school he had attended in Berkeley, California—Starr King, a Unitarian Universalist seminary. He said it was an institution that said a radical "yes!" to those students they chose to admit. At that point, I could certainly use a "yes." *Maybe I should consider seminary, I thought. I had always been religious, after all.*

# 6

# *Starr King*

*Faith is the bird that feels the light when the dawn is still dark.*
—RABINDRANATH TAGORE, *FIREFLIES*, 1928

So I flew out to California for the first time in my life, flew into that strange land called Berkeley to interview at Starr King. I remember the interview well. One lay member of the committee asked me, "What will you do if we don't accept you?"

I said, "I don't know."

Next, I was interviewed by a professor, Ron Cook. Ron was a rangy and unnervingly frank fellow with a crooked smile that broke through now and then. He asked me, "What is your goal in life?" Nothing like starting with the big questions.

I blurted out, "I want to be all used up."

He said, "Well, parish ministry should do that for you."

Before I left Berkeley, the school told me I had been accepted. But should I go? Deeply conflicted, I flew back home to think it over. I wasn't sure I wanted to become a parish minister, yet I knew I needed to heal, to find my way. I needed the "yes" like the one Starr King promised. *But what about my boys? How could I possibly leave them?*

One morning about two weeks after I returned home, I was awakened before dawn. Something, some internal voice, told me to get dressed and go for a walk. Getting up at that hour is not something I would ever, ever consider my own free will. I generally go to bed late, get up late—I've never seen a sunrise unless forced to by some early plane I had to catch. But I knew I must obey this voice. I got up, put on my jeans and my jacket, and walked out into the dark. I walked without a destination, just one step after the next, ending up at Transylvania, a nearby university.

The campus was a broad expanse of green with one small tree in sight. I walked toward the tree, the darkness giving way to light, and I saw there among the branches a little brown bird. I moved closer and closer to the tree, in the eerie silence of the early morning, until I was standing right next to the bird. Strangely, *it did not fly away*. I stayed with the bird for a few minutes, then walked back home. Without thinking—just moving automatically—I got out my ancient portable typewriter and composed my acceptance letter to Starr King.

What was this all about? I don't know. All I can do is report my experience. Much later in seminary, however, I was casually thumbing through a dictionary of religious symbols, and it hit me—of course! The bird is the traditional symbol of the Spirit. I remembered the dove descending when Jesus was baptized, the dove that told Noah land was near. My little bird was not so dramatic or so imposing—just a little sparrow, most likely, hovering in the dark and waiting for the dawn.

Years later, I recounted this experience to my son Madison during a road trip we were taking together, one of those out-of-time occasions that invite thoughts of the heart. He was in college at the time with a triple major in mathematics, physics, and logic, so I was a bit reluctant to tell the story, anticipating that he might be skeptical. When I finished the telling, I paused dramatically and waited. He said, "Mom, that's the stupidest thing I've ever heard." Maybe so, but I bet my life on it.

Several months later, I left for Berkeley on the Sunset Limited, with a suitcase, two boxes of books, and my two sons. They were to live with their father and stepmother in Kentucky, but I took them with me on the initial trip to California because they were still so young, nine and ten, and I didn't want them to see their mother just get on a plane and disappear: I wanted them to know, geographically at least, where I was going to be.

The boys and I made a couple of stops—El Paso, where I bought them smooth leather billfolds and handmade blankets, small enough to fold and put in their suitcases. I also bought a creche set, with its dark-skinned Baby Jesus, which I still take out every Christmas. We had a long layover in San Diego, where we went to Sea World (pre-*Free Willy*), and saw the orcas slice through the water, leap up, and grab a fish from the trainer's mouth. We watched as a pearl diver went down in fifteen feet of water, brought up an oyster, opened it with a smile, and as the three of us looked on expectantly, lifted a good-sized pearl from the shell. The boys said they were going to give it to their stepmother, as a peace offering, I presume, because she hadn't wanted them to move in. But I told them I wanted it, had to have it. I cried. They didn't quite understand why, but they gave it to me. *The pearl of great price.*

We arrived in San Francisco, spent the night with the brother of a friend, my only contact in the Bay Area, and the next morning I put them on the plane back to Kentucky. I was stunned. Later, I couldn't stop crying. Many nights that first year in seminary, my pillow was wet with tears. I missed my boys, and they missed me. At first, we sent tapes back and forth. I still have that first tape, with Madison's sad, innocent voice saying, "When are you coming to see us, Mommy?" He still didn't understand the vast distance. Broke my heart. Still does.

As with any decision, there is a cost—you make a choice: there is the road taken, and there is the road not taken and yes, my choice did make all the difference. My sons and I used to regularly play Marlo Thomas's "Free to Be You and Me," leaping around on the vast blue carpet in the living room, celebrating life, possibility. I wanted them to grow up free from gender stereotypes, free to become whatever might be calling them—and I wanted freedom for myself. That song revealed my yearning, and always brought tears. I was breaking free.

Kash and Madison were with me during Christmas and again each summer during my seminary years, and Madison spent his last two years of high school with me in Berkeley. Their father was, and is, a good and loving man. But they had to contend with their stepmother and the absence of their mother. She made no secret that she didn't want them there. Let's have no bullshit about "my courageous decision to upend my marriage and go to seminary": my sons paid quite a price for my freedom.

# 7

# *Searching*

Many people have a hallowed, even romantic view of ministry. When a fellow passenger on a plane asks me in hushed tones, "Why did you decide to become a minister?" I answer, "It was the money." On the surface, that was true—but my experience at seminary offered so much ripening, so much more than a way to make a living. I thought I would be in Berkeley for three years—it turned out to be eight, four for the MDiv and four for a PhD in theology and literature. Madison and I graduated together, he from Berkeley High School and me with my doctorate from the Graduate Theological Union and the University of California at Berkeley.

Thus began what became a long and frustrating search for a pulpit. In ministry, we speak of a *call*—that is, the match between a minister and a church, grounded in a spiritual sense that they are right for each other. Ministers are in service to something larger than themselves—at least, that's the ideal. They depend on partnering with the Spirit that led them into ministry, and they seek a post that is congruent with who they are and what they can offer. Woe to those ministers who choose a church for the salary or geographical location, for they are often doomed to failure.

Unitarian Universalist churches are congregationally based, so each church chooses its own minister in a lengthy process. Finalists go through a pre-candidating process, which includes three days of interviews with the search committee, followed by a Sunday preaching event at a nearby church. Generally, churches will ask two to four ministers to pre-candidate and then choose one as their candidate. That minister visits for a week with church committees and leaders and staff, and preaches two sermons, one at the beginning, the other at the end of the week. Then the congregation votes.

My quest for a pulpit did not go well. In the final year of my doctoral studies, I did five three-day interviews all over the country, from Florida to California, but no church seemed right for me. The head of the Unitarian Universalist Placement Department was irritated—he told me I was "being aloof" with these churches. I told him I did not feel called—*didn't he understand the concept of a call, I wondered*. I asked to do an interim ministry for a year. Soon I began receiving slips of paper in the mail, letting me know of churches looking for an interim. I kept throwing them in the trash. *What is wrong with me?*

Then one day, a slip came suggesting the First Unitarian Church in Cincinnati. I knew instantly that I must go to Cincinnati—this was another one of those choices driven by internal necessity. Without thinking, I called up the head of the interim search committee and said I wanted to take the position. I couldn't articulate why I felt compelled to go there, but later it hit me: Cincinnati was, of course, the city where my family was living when Daddy took us children so abruptly from our mother.

*One day in July, Big Papa and Uncle Gene appeared at our white frame house in Cincinnati. Mother wasn't home. Daddy spread a sheet on the floor, pulled out drawers, dumped our clothes inside. Then he tied up the sheet and threw it in the trunk of Big Papa's black Studebaker.*

*I left a room of my own and my own bed with my patent leather shoes neatly tucked underneath. I left my "box of secrets" in its hiding place. We couldn't take my puppy, Daddy said, just the clothes. Not my big bride doll, either.*

*My brother and sister and I crowded into the car, and Uncle Gene drove fast, out of Cincinnati, into the countryside, across the river on a small railroad bridge with no rails, on across the state line to Kentucky, on toward Louisiana.*

*I was nine years old. I didn't see my mother again until I graduated from college.*

*We children were not told where our mother was or why she was absent from our lives. We didn't ask about her. We sensed from our father's troubled eyes that the past was best left behind. We followed blindly, trusting our caretakers, as children are wont to do. Only years later, as adults, we learned our mother had been sent to a mental hospital, where she stayed for a year.*

......

Of course, a mother cannot be left behind. My mother's absence had always been a great presence in my life—I was not ready for a call as yet. I spent that year serving First Unitarian—and at the same time seeing a psychiatrist, Madeline, who guided me as I worked through buried feelings about losing my mother.

One day I brought in a crayon drawing I had done. It was abstract, all in slashing red streaks. "What does red mean to you?" Madeline asked.

"Love," I said. "Passion, maybe."

"What about anger?" she said. *Yes, what about anger.* To avoid visiting that anger on some congregation, I needed to acknowledge it in myself, to look at the source. And to see what was driving my drifts into depression.

As Madeline helped me push through long-held defenses, I had times of emotional flooding that left me unable to focus. But I was more alive and present than ever, and the church was a healthy one with strong lay leadership, so my ministry flourished. I continued my search for a church, doing four more pre-candidatings. I was becoming apt at interviewing, and churches wanted me. But I was quite sure I did not want them. *Why was nothing working out?* I began questioning whether or not I was even supposed to be a minister. I wouldn't be the first ministerial student who gets a degree and then finds *whoops, parish ministry is not my calling.*

Then the chair of the search committee at First Unitarian Church in Portland, Oregon, called and asked me to pre-candidate. This was the tenth and last church I looked at. The call came as I was preparing to fly to Louisiana—my father had just died. Mother, father gone. I fell into melancholy, a lament for my parents' helpless, hapless longing for each other, for their unrequited love. At the same time, I felt a cutting loose. A new era was about to begin.

# 8

# *Finding*

As the plane circled Portland International Airport, I took in the seemingly boundless miles of deep green that characterize Oregon. Upon arriving, I was greeted by a couple of members of the search committee, who took me on a tour of the city. I saw the sturdy, well-built cottages, the craftsman homes in the historic district. Trees everywhere, and flowers—the Rose City was awash in color: rhododendrons, azaleas, tulips, daffodils.

Next, I was taken to the church. The sanctuary was a classic New England structure, reflecting the heritage of the founders, prominent individuals from the East who established the church in 1866—the second Unitarian church on the West Coast, the first after San Francisco. The elegant and beautifully appointed sanctuary was designed by architect Jamieson K. Parker and built in 1927, the third incarnation of the church since 1867, when a small chapel was built, just 50 by 60 feet, in a city that had only 5,000 or so inhabitants. The interior of the Parker Chapel said *beauty*, said *history*, said *worship*. And the church was in the heart of the city, where great churches are located, downtown amid the commerce and amid those who did not partake of the commerce— the runaway teen, the needle users, those with no home. A quotation from Mic. 6:8 appears on the north side of the building, setting forth the purpose of the founders: "And what does the Lord require of you? To act justly and to love mercy and to walk humbly with your God." When I left the sanctuary, bathed in a late-afternoon light that captured a sense of the sacred, I knew I wanted to be part of the tradition of this historic church.

At the end of my first interview with the search committee, I looked at them one by one and said, with absolute assurance, "This is where I'm called to be." I'm not sure how I knew, for there is a great mystery about a call, but at that moment, I had an internal conviction that would not be shaken, not then, not ever. Since a search committee generally invites a candidate, not vice versa, my declaration precipitated a good deal of polite coughing. Finally, someone asked, "And why do you think so?"

My response rolled off my tongue. After all, the words had been waiting two years to be spoken. "I can offer you some things that you need," I said. "I'm a strong preacher, and a large church needs a strong preacher." I paused, then went on. "More important, you are a great church, and you have forgotten this. I can help you remember that you are great." I paused again, to let my promise sink in, then continued. "And you can give me something I need: I need to be challenged to excellence, and you can do that for me." Where did these thoughts come from? Hard to say. I just know I felt the truth of those declarations in my very core.

Now this is the strange thing: *I knew I would be selected*—against all logic and precedence. I was untried as a minister, and this was a large church. The only reason I was one of the candidates is that the placement director at the Unitarian Universalist Association, seeking to be inclusive, needed a woman along with the four men they suggested, and I was a woman with a PhD. Over the long weeks of waiting for the church's decision, I had tried to prepare myself that I would not be chosen, *no, no, surely not*, but I couldn't shake the strong sense that, in fact, I would be. Two months later, the chair of the search committee called to invite me to candidate as their minister. I didn't feel the exhilaration, the sudden thrill one might expect: I merely accepted what I knew was a foregone conclusion. I never doubted throughout my seventeen years of ministry that the church and I were in a covenantal relationship that was meant to be.

This is not to say that everyone accepted the decision of the search committee. After all, I was the first female senior minister after a long line of male leaders, whose photos proudly adorned a single long wall. One of the members of the committee itself, a long-established lawyer, lobbied against me with the older members of the power structure. Most of our ministers expect 98 or even 100 percent, for the congregation generally trusts the decision of the search committee. I had decided that if I received 90 percent of the votes, I would accept the call. I received 93 percent, as I remember. When the vote was tallied, the lawyer challenged the results, saying that not enough people were in the room where the votes were counted. He did not prevail, and the church issued a call.

I had arrived at exactly the right place. This was not the Northeast, where people ask you where you went to boarding school. This was not the South, where family counted above all. This was not the Midwest, steeped in strong values but unable to imagine new ways. No, this was the Pacific Northwest, where anything was possible, where the only relevant question is: Do you have the right stuff?

The installation service was at the First Methodist Church, for our sanctuary was not large enough for the event. It was a grand occasion, attended by the mayor, the president of Reed College, and various dignitaries from the denomination. But my greatest joy that evening was the presence of Kash and Madison in their suits, college boys now, all grown up. My work had taken me from them. And it continued to do so for many years as I led a growing institution. They have had both to forgive me and to celebrate me, which I believe on both accounts they have largely done.

# 9

# *Coming into My Own*

> 'Tis the gift to be simple, 'tis the gift to be free
> 'tis the gift to come down where I ought to be
> And when we find ourselves in the place just right
> 'Twill be in the valley of love and delight.
> — "SIMPLE GIFTS," BY ELDER JOSEPH BRACKET

First Unitarian, like most other churches, thrived in certain periods and in others, struggled. I arrived at a church that had fallen on hard times. Morale was low, finances insecure. So there was institutional work to be done, and a lot of it. Membership numbers were inexact, but there were approximately 600–650 congregants. Outside of the half-time music director, the religious education director, and the long-time church secretary, the staff were semi-volunteers with token salaries. The secretary had long functioned as the administrator of the church. No one on staff had health insurance.

I remembered my brazen promise to the search committee: I would help them remember their remarkable history and reaffirm their sense of purpose and leadership in the community. I didn't know whether or not I could deliver. I had never led an institution, had never held an administrative post. With so little experience, I was leading blindly—and so was pushed to a deeper faith. I made mistakes, as any beginner does. But I knew why I was there, and I knew where my strength was tethered. I trusted that if my call was right and I clung fast to my partnership with the Spirit, the congregation and I would flourish together.

I had never been to Portland before my interview, so I began my ministry with not a single friend or even an acquaintance. My first act after finding a place to live was to search out a therapist—I had to tell someone about the doubts and fears churning inside. Parish ministry is a difficult profession with a high drop-out rate—ministers are vulnerable as they try to guide their congregants into realms of truth and justice and at the same time draw a salary from these same people. As John Buehrens, my intern director, said, "You best keep your bags packed. If your vision and the church's vision become different, it's time to leave." Through my years of ministry, I saw many fine, deeply committed ministers forced out of their churches for one reason or another. It can happen to anyone.

I was fortunate—First Unitarian and I were beautifully matched: my theology was inclusive enough for the congregation, and my political persuasions were way to the left, a perfect fit for progressive Portland. The congregation and I were meant for each other in some fateful way.

Needless to say, though, I had a lot to learn about ministry. My challenges were complicated by the rapid growth of the congregation. Early in my ministry—in fact, before I ever stepped into the pulpit—forces of hate and division in Oregon had created a state ballot measure seeking to overturn the civil rights of gays and lesbians. As a public witness, we wrapped the church block with a red ribbon, declared ourselves a Hate Free Zone, and called a press conference.

The press conference drew just about every media outlet in Portland. It just so happened that the monthly meeting of the Women's Alliance was taking place at that very time, and so forty or fifty most elderly women came outside and joined the fray—yes, gray hairs supporting gay rights! An appealing combination for progressive Portland. This one event challenged the largely unchurched Portlanders' stereotypical ideas about religion. Our growth was jump-started—we soon became the church "where it was at," not only for a flood of gays and lesbians but also for people who had given up on mainline churches or who described themselves as "spiritual, but not religious." We grew 40 percent in my first year.

Overwhelmed, leading a church that was way, way under-resourced for this growth, I became radically dependent upon the God that brought me to

Portland. Not that anyone can claim to know absolutely that God exists. But I knew *I* wasn't God, and that's the only place to begin. If I was truly called, I knew I would be held. And I was held during all of my seventeen years of ministry in Portland.

My work began by helping the congregation clarify the church's mission. Why did the church exist? Surely not just to serve ourselves as a social center. We did a mission study over a period of many months. A synthesis of our efforts was eventually expressed this way: "Our mission is to grow spiritually and bless the larger world." I had to build a professional staff, which required the congregation to substantially increase their giving—historically, they had been reluctant to discuss money openly and had existed perpetually in a culture of scarcity. We began the shift to a culture of plenty. And people came. Money came.

The rapid growth of the church, coupled with my inexperience, made for a rocky transition, but the center held, and the church continued to increase in numbers and influence. I never developed the skills to read a spreadsheet—I left that to the financial manager. My philosophy about money was simple—we always needed more, and I kept asking for more. We had to build an infrastructure to handle the numbers of people who were pouring through our doors. One consultant we hired described us as "a giant vacuum cleaner with no bag attached."

The church was filled to bursting on Sunday morning, and we were straining to welcome those who wanted to join us. We rescued an abandoned church at the end of our block and took our expanding numbers there—I did three services on a Sunday for five years, and so did the choirs, the Sunday school, and the ushers.

Next, we expanded the sanctuary so we could hold 500 worshippers in each of two services. We retrofitted the original historic sanctuary to prevent a potential earthquake from flattening the building—and began calling it a chapel. The church complex, though, had become a rabbit warren, difficult to negotiate, especially for newcomers. Worse, the 400 children in our religious education program had long been meeting in what was essentially a fire trap: the third story of an old wooden building. They needed a safe space. So we had to create a vision and then lay plans for a new building. In my naivete, I thought the whole process would take about three years: one to set the architecture, another to raise the money, and a third to build the building. It took thirteen.

The church eventually had 1,600 members and a new three-story educational building, not just for the congregation's children on Sunday morning, but also for a vast array of adult classes for spiritual growth, offering everything from Buddhist meditation to yoga to Shakespeare. Our new building became a center for the larger community, sponsoring conferences and workshops on a wide variety of justice issues. Four hundred of our congregants went into the street to protest the bombing that started the Iraq war. We welcomed writers and speakers, including Paul Krugman, Matthew Fox, Susan Griffin, David Cay Johnson, Denise Levertov. The church had become known in Portland as a place where people "walk their talk," or so our newcomers often said.

I arrived in Portland inexperienced and uncertain, hoping I could fulfill the promise I had made to the search committee. Now, seventeen years later, I was leaving the church and the community I loved and served. I had completed my covenant with them. It was time to go.

*II*

# Falling

# 10

# *Losing*

There are days in our lives when everything changes: the wedding day, as you hear yourself making the ancient promises; your ecstatic joy the moment your first newborn is placed in your arms; the time you hear the betrayal that sends you spinning out of control. I remember so well the intimate details of the morning before I preached my last sermon at the church. My confused heart asking *am I making a mistake?*; my morning prayer asking for guidance—*what's next?* Slowly, carefully dressing: the white silk shirt with the bow at the neck and the long sash; the practical black skirt, my Sunday costume to go under the red doctoral robe with the black velvet panel, the robe that said *something very special is about to happen here*. The sweet energy of coming together one last time. The sermon, my blessing, given in love. And then the aftermath of the service: the emptiness of the church after the last hug was given, the robe slowly peeled off, the final sermon tucked back in its manila folder, along with the order of service, as was my custom.

······

The associate minister, Tom Disrud, was chosen to lead the church during a year of transition while a search was underway for a new senior minister. I was named Minister Emerita—nevertheless, I was not to attend any services in the sanctuary, nor attend community meetings held in the church, nor so much as enter the church property for any reason whatsoever for two calendar years. According to our consultant, my absence would support the authority of the interim and would encourage congregants to bond with the new minister when that position was filled.

I agreed to these terms for the supposed good of the institution—but in retrospect, I realize I was naïve about the emotional fallout for me, as well as the confusion and loss felt by many in the congregation. *She has baptized our babies, buried our parents, and now we can't talk to her? She's here one day and absolutely gone the next?* In a moment, I was changed from one who comforts to one who endangers. Some ministers have referred to this practice as "a ministry of absence," surely an Orwellian term.

I felt as though I had been banned, shunned. The church is downtown, so I had cause to pass it frequently, often finding my face wet with tears. On Christmas Eve, I was forbidden to attend the service. *Silent night, holy night, all is calm, all is bright.* The congregants would be singing, holding candles to fend off the dark. I was despondent.

I had been uprooted from just about everything that gave my life meaning: my way of giving, my ability to exercise power, my role as a spiritual leader. And I had become separated from the community of people I loved, the body of people who had held me fast through the years and made legitimate my work in the world. *What was the meaning and purpose of my life now?* The question reverberated throughout my system.

*I feel a pain in my heel. I find the tip of something hard protruding from the surface of the heel. I get a pair of tweezers, grasp the offending object, start to pull. I am shocked at how long it is. I keep pulling and pulling. Finally, it comes out. It is an inch-long needle.*

・・・・・・

Some retired ministers seem to adjust with little or no trouble. Others experience a good deal of emotional pain when they leave, especially those who've had a strong ministry over many years of service. Some quit the community altogether, trying to avoid the issue. Much depends upon the ministers involved, their avocations and interests, their history with the church, and of course their own personal history. I've tried to sort out why I responded so acutely to leaving the church. Surely part of my difficulty could be explained by the trauma in my early life. I decided to seek counseling from a psychiatrist. I told him about the time my father kidnapped my little brother and sister and me and took us from our mother. He described my current condition as post-traumatic stress disorder. Retirement had triggered my abandonment issues. We worked together each week for many years.

# 11

## *Growing-Up Days*

My parents, Jim and Marion, were star-crossed lovers. Marion was a big city girl, a former dancer who traveled all over the United States with a show company, starting when she was thirteen. Jim was a rural boy, tied to the earth and small-town life. They met in Washington, D.C., during the Depression, where they both had gone seeking work. He was a handsome waiter in a German restaurant, she a charming customer.

I was the eldest child, born in Washington in 1941. Soon after my birth, the family retreated to Cincinnati, where my mother had a large extended family. Aunt Florence, married to my mother's brother, tended to me during those early months of my life. According to her, "Marion was too agitated to care for you—you would cry every time she tried to hold you." My mother was described as "schizophrenic," but that seems to have been the blanket term in those days for anyone mentally ill. I'm guessing that my mother suffered from severe postpartum depression.

*Your mother cried and pushed you away, her breasts hurting with the milk that refused to flow, she pinched and prodded, but the breasts stayed hard to the touch, you tried and tried to suck and screamed, cried for the milk that refused to come, you decided even then, even as a newborn, that you were ruined, like milk tainted with a crimson drop of iodine or blood that holds for a second, then merges and stains through and through.*

· · · · · ·

When I was still a baby, our family moved to my father's hometown, Homer, Louisiana, which Mother described as "that hick town." She begged my father to move back to Cincinnati—she wanted to be near the bright lights of the city and her family. He finally relented. He found a job in a candy factory, coming home from work with pockets full of candy for us kids, who were three in number by then. That work must have been anathema to him, a highly skilled oil field worker who had worked on rigs all over north Louisiana and east Texas.

I don't know all the circumstances that led our father to snatch us and take us to Louisiana to live with his parents. My father said that Mother was headed for another mental breakdown—and she was plotting to divorce him and take us children. A few months before she died, Mother told me that my father had been having an affair. No one in either my mother's or my father's family seems to have a clear hold on the truth. There were, I expect, many truths, depending upon one's perspective. Family secrets hover 'round like ghosts, affecting so many lives, ever elusive. *What really happened? Whose story is to be believed?*

There in Louisiana, my father turned to alcohol and women to assuage his grief—eventually he was married a total of five times, each marriage being interrupted by his drinking. It was when he was drunk that he would speak of our mother, his eyes filling with tears: "I love your mother. How could I not? She's the mother of you children." Neither time nor distance nor suffering could make either of them forget. Though apart for the last thirty years of their lives, each fell into sadness at the mention of the other's name. My father died in a state mental hospital in Louisiana, of alcohol dementia. For the last years of his life, he was not able to recognize his own children—his children and hers. As for Mother, she said she never looked at another man. "How could I, after your father?" As she neared death, she begged me, "Ask your father to call." He never did. He couldn't. But after she died, he sat at my kitchen table with his face in his hands, weeping without measure.

......

My grandparents were generous beyond words—I understand that now—taking in three children and their wayward son. But they were too old to parent. The rules of the household were laid down, strict and clear: "obey your elders, do your schoolwork, go to church, don't talk back." And in particular for me, young bookworm that I was, "stop your reading and be in bed by 9:00 p.m." (in order to save on electricity). My father was off at the oil rig. When he got home, he cleaned up, scrubbing his blackened skin, washing his hair of the sand and oil, leaving the washing machine full of grit, and then driving out of town to see his current girlfriend. When work was slow, he would lie in the back bedroom, under the black walnut tree, smoking Picayune cigarettes and reading *True Detective*. If empty days stretched on, he would become restless and go on a drinking binge. Sometimes we didn't know where he was for days at a time, then eventually he would come back, staggering through the front door. We'd fry him up a half-dozen eggs and some bacon; he would eat and fall into bed. My grandfather, Big Papa, would shake his head and say, "James, James!" My grandmother would pray. We three children would be sad and silent.

Black women filled in where care was missing. Our little town of 5,000 had 2,000 whites and 3,000 Blacks. Blacks were relegated to their own neighborhoods. There was little employment available for them, just farm work for the men and domestic work for the women. Our family was relatively poor when judged against the families of my school friends, but a Black woman worked in our home five days a week. Three different women filled that role: Christine, large and silent, as durable as stone; then Marguerite, young and thin and pretty; later Ida, who wore a red kerchief wrapped around her head and told us kids ghost stories. They cooked, they ironed, they cleaned.

I remember asking Marguerite about boys, in tears: "Marguerite, will I ever have a boyfriend, a real boyfriend?" Marguerite looked at me straight on and said, "Ain't you the strangest thing! A'course you will. You be gettin' prettier every day. You gonna have all the boyfriends you want, more probably than you wanna put up with." Years later, when I returned home for my grandmother's funeral, I saw Christine in the balcony of First Baptist, sitting there alone. She was a presence like the earth itself.

First Baptist Church was the spiritual and social center of our community—the tall yellow brick building was perched up on a hill catty-corner from Pee Wee's filling station, where my father got his bootleg whiskey. I had concluded, as children will, that if no one saw to my needs, I must somehow be at fault.

I saw myself as inherently unlovable, as being flawed in some way I couldn't describe, for which there was no remedy. Like most of my friends, I attended church three times a week—twice on Sunday and again on Wednesday evening. If I couldn't be loved, I could at least be *good*, I could be *smart*. It was at church and at school where I felt accepted, even honored.

I coped with my depression and anxiety by staying in school most of my adult life, drawing praise and piling up virtue, eventually getting four graduate degrees. Later, my refuge was work: teacher, clinical social worker, minister. I was taking care of others, aping the care I needed for myself. It is definitely more blessed to give than to receive, especially if receiving is fraught with difficulty.

I have a photo of myself at the time of my first communion. I am dressed in lacy white, with a veil, clutching my white prayer book. My body is rigid, my legs like sticks, I'm staring straight at the camera. Another photo, a family picture taken when I was nine—I am looking up at my mother, who has a broad smile, which doesn't hint at the fact that she is soon to have another mental breakdown. I am grasping a little white beaded purse with both hands. A third photo, this one of me at age sixty. The photographer is a professional, a friend of mine. He has taken hundreds of pictures of me over many years' time. This photograph is the finest of all, the one he often exhibits when he does shows. The top of the photo begins with my shoulders; below, a pearl necklace appears on a classic neckline, and as a viewer's eyes move down, the focus is on the hands. They are clenching the handle of a small white vintage purse. *I am such a good girl.*

# 12

# *Grieving*

Thomas Moore writes in his book *Ageless Soul*, "neurotic suffering can be healed through service and reaching out beyond yourself." Works for me. Pay attention to the suffering of others. Or simply pay attention to others. And the relentless ragging of the brain, the solipsistic wanderings of the mind, stop.

So what is this "neurotic suffering" Moore speaks of? All kinds of imbalances show up in the human nervous system: one person is anxious and jumpy, another has a flat affect, a third is too quick on the trigger, a fourth stays spaced out, dreaming, too much of the time. Some of these tendencies are built-in, genetically. Our environment kicks in at birth, and we form personality patterns. Some of these are adaptive, bringing joy and purpose, others leave us unsettled, troubled. To some extent, all dysfunctional behaviors are responses to the fear of abandonment. To belong to the tribe is to survive. To put it simply, we never stop needing love.

An unmarried minister is an anomaly: if a minister loses a spouse, they find another. Marriage avoids awkward interactions with single congregants. And spouses offer support, not only needed because of long days of work but essential when church conflicts arise, which they inevitably do. I longed for a partner. I remember asking a well-connected lawyer on the board why no one was introducing me to men I might date. I'll never forget his response: "I think we're afraid that if you get married, you'll leave us." So they thought my call would be tossed aside if I fell in love? Not a message that would ever have been given to a male minister.

I needed care, of course, and so I secured that in whatever ways I could. My associate minister, Tom Disrud, became a dear friend, as well as performing his professional role. He was a gay man and single, and we spent most every holiday together, including Christmas Day. Done with the pressures of the season, including the Christmas Eve service, we met at his home the following morning, where we opened gifts from family members and from each other. Tom was an exceptional cook and host, so he took charge of the requisite dinners and parties for church leaders—traditionally the purview of the minister's wife. We worked together as a team, and I could not have led the church successfully without him. He filled in where I was weak, and his caring presence was always there for me. Interestingly, he finally found a relationship just as I was leaving the church, as did I. The church is an exceedingly jealous mistress.

In fact, I had a whole raft of caretakers: my primary care physician, a psychiatrist, a spiritual director, and a massage therapist who brought his table to my home each Sunday after I preached and lulled my tired body to sleep. I had a house cleaner, a gardener, a handyman. They all were part of the community that sustained me, saw to my needs, fed my hunger. I couldn't have functioned without them.

It all worked so well—then the church was abruptly gone. Though I had chosen to leave, I felt abandoned—the same way I always felt when I broke up a relationship. *Why did you leave me? Oh, I forgot—I left you.*

Loss is visceral, and logic is no buffer. Each loss reminds us of earlier losses. The childhood friend moves away. The grandmother dies. A parent dies or disappears. Those early losses never completely heal, and they can be triggered by new circumstances all through life. The ferocious energy of loss is surprising, and grieving is ever a necessity through the many transitions of our lives.

But expressing grief is not done easily in our culture. The pattern is to ignore the grief, to appear strong, not a "crybaby." In fact, after having seen too many David Attenborough films, I wonder if it is almost instinctual not to appear weak, for we see in the animal kingdom the weak and the sick being taken down by predators. The grieving become "other," difficult to be around, for they remind us of our own losses, our own fears. Some friends are strong and mature enough to leave the door of honesty open, many are not.

Typically, when I ask a retiree about their adjustment to leaving work, they will begin with some ultra-positive statement about their newfound freedom from demands, their plans for trips or other pleasures put on hold. But with very little probing, many begin to confess the loss involved, the emptiness they experience. The work of grieving cries out to be done.

# 13

## *Looking for Home*

When I retired, I knew that my greatest risk was isolation. Because parish ministry is so all-encompassing, I had done little to create and nurture friendships outside of church. The church gave me quite enough contact with people, and when work was done, I gladly retreated to my comfortable nest, my refuge of silence. My home had become a kind of monastery, with no music, no TV or radio. I retreated to my blessed words—reading and writing.

My house was typical of the area: it was built in the early 1900s, a classic two-story craftsman, with a broad front porch. Every afternoon or evening I took a walk, alone, in the tree-lined streets of the historic neighborhood where I had put down roots. In spring, lush flowers beckoned from every well-kept yard; in the winter, the stark skeletons of trees held the ground secure.

Sometimes dusk fell before I'd arrive home, and I would pass the lighted interiors of other houses, see the lace at the windows, people sitting in comfortable chairs, perhaps a dining room with a chandelier. I would fantasize about the lives of the people, imagine they were warm and happy, imagine what it might be like to be returning home to someone. At times I felt the want of company, but in truth, I tolerated my aloneness well. I knew I had chosen it, and it had its rich rewards, not the least of which was building the institution I led, making a space for many to find a spiritual home.

On the other hand, without my work and the everyday interactions with my congregants and staff, I knew I would be lost. As I prepared to retire, I began thinking of where I would go, what city, what kind of living arrangement. I could not live alone, I knew, for I was prone to depression, and should

I become isolated, dark moods would threaten not just my joy but my very survival. So I went in search.

Maybe I would return to Lexington, Kentucky, where I raised my children and where I still had good friends. Maybe I would buy a charming home in Fairhope, Alabama, a little arts community where my sister lived. Or maybe Durham, North Carolina, where there was a strong Unitarian Universalist church led by a minister friend of mine. Or in Hillsborough, a small historic town near Durham where several writers had settled, including Allan Gurganus and Jill McCorkle. I visited there and chatted with folks at the Cup A Joe coffeehouse. Nothing was quite right.

What about staying in Portland, where my work was known and I had a few close friends? I could find a shared living situation, I thought. I checked out a planned community on the outskirts of town, where everyone had their own private space, interacting for cooking and eating and various projects and committees. No. I'd had enough of meetings and didn't want that kind of structured life. Too much, too close, I decided.

Next I visited Mike, an acquaintance who was a well-known environmental activist. He had created a living situation in a fourplex with three other friends who were activists of one kind or another. He told me that for him it was ideal—he had his own apartment, but he could stop in for a drink or a meal from time to time with the others, and sometimes all the residents hosted a party for mutual friends. That model of living sounded right for me. I could sell my home and buy a bigger space in a less expensive area and invite others of like mind to live alongside me. There were potential drawbacks, though: it wouldn't be egalitarian because I would be their landlady, managing the space—more power and responsibility than I wanted. If we all bought part of the building, the way Mike and his friends did, then there would be the problem of trying to sell the space when an individual or couple wanted to move out. Or maybe I would want to move at some point because of health issues or other considerations. Just sounded problematic.

What about moving to a Continuing Care Retirement Community, or CCRC, as an old friend suggested? There's a big market for CCRCs now that baby boomers are aging, with more and more people living well into their nineties and even longer. CCRCs generally have three levels of care: independent living, in which residents are offered group activities and enjoy amenities such as a fitness center and warm pool; assisted living, in which residents are given help as needed with daily tasks, such as bathing and dressing; and nursing care provided around the clock for those whose health is fragile.

I had, through the years, done pastoral care in many of these institutions, and I always came away depressed. The quiet good taste of the foyer, the decorative paintings of country scenes, the empty stuffed chairs, and the artificial flowers, followed by the elevators, the long hallways, the dining hall with no young or even middle-aged people. CRCCs are currently changing, appealing to younger folks who want to engage in all kinds of activities, from reading groups to pickleball, so maybe one day this setting might appeal to me. Residents "stay around some seven or ten years," one article said—no doubt the writer meant "before they die," but death is not spoken of. I wasn't ready to move into such a place—at least, not yet.

So I found myself unsure of where to go, how to imagine a future for myself. Nothing seemed to work. I had to find an answer—no small dilemma.

# 14

## *Surprised by Joy*

I had long admired architect George Crandall, a member of our church. George had lived and worked in Portland for thirty-five years, and much of the beauty and livability of the city can be laid to his vision. He designed "Big Pink," a landmark tower, a parallelogram shimmering with pink Spanish granite that changes color according to the light of each moment of the day. He was also in charge of the restoration of the magnificent downtown library, overseeing the design of every jot and tittle of the building, inside and out. Then he went on to found Crandall Arambula, a firm with the singular focus of revitalizing cities.

George was one of those individuals for whom everything seemed to turn round right. I was shocked, then, to hear of the sudden death of Ann, his wife of forty-seven years. I called and we spoke briefly. He was devastated, barely coherent. I wrote a letter of consolation, inviting him to talk, if he felt that might help. I didn't expect him to be open to my offer—he's one who gives help, not needs help. Gracious, always the gentleman, he's a man who carries a white handkerchief, pressed and ready to proffer should a lady find herself in tears. Old school. But he surprised me by saying he did want to meet, that he didn't know what to do with his grief. I knew he wouldn't be comfortable coming to my church office for "counseling," so I suggested that we meet at the Heathman Hotel in their elegant tearoom. For an hour, over many cups of tea, he poured out his story. I listened. It's what ministers do: provide an opening for whatever needs to be felt or said.

George gave a step-by-step account of how Ann suddenly became ill, how what seemed controllable was not, the missteps at the hospital, the call in the night. Then his story seemed to come to an end. He paused. He looked at me. He said, "What are you doing these days?" A most peculiar question to ask of a minister giving pastoral care. Entirely inappropriate.

I finessed a response, "Oh, I love my work, keeps me busy," and turned the conversation back to him. He would have none of it.

Rephrasing his question, he said, "What are you excited about?"

Flustered, I blurted out, "Do you really want to know?"

"Yes, I want to know what you're interested in." George has a way of meaning what he says.

"Well . . . I'm making a film. A documentary. I'm, uh, the subject."

He smiled for the first time in our conversation. "That could be great fun—or you might just flame out."

I laughed. "Yes, you're right."

"And that would be OK."

I loved the honesty, the self-confidence, the security embodied in that remark. *Yes, I might flame out, and it would be OK.* Everything shifted. I started telling him about the film, the impetus for it, the process of filmmaking itself. We became just two people talking with each other about our lives. He touched my arm to emphasize a point. I felt free to touch him. Toward the end of our time together, he looked at me, shy, like a schoolboy, then glanced down. *He just fell in love with me.*

I knew when I left the hotel that day that I would marry him. I was stunned, unbelieving. But a kind of deep knowing had asserted itself and would not be shaken. It was too soon, of course, way too soon. But love doesn't play by the rules. When it shows up, we do well to pay attention.

I began almost immediately to question myself. Maybe this is a fantasy, my little trip into wish fulfillment. Will he come for me, or will he disappear? I needed to back off and let him take the initiative—or not.

George asked me for some reading to help him through the grieving process, so one day I dropped off a couple of books at his office, timing my visit when I knew he wouldn't be there. He would have to make the next move, if there was to be one. He called a few days later and began a forty-five-minute monologue, reviewing the content of the books. Clearly, he had read both books carefully and digested them. And clearly, his interest was in talking with me, not in the books. I knew he was stalling. He paused. Silence. Finally, he squeezed out the words: "I'd like . . . to see you."

Aware of the ambiguity possible in his statement, I took a long, quiet moment and then said, "And how would you like to do that?"

George said, "I'd like to take you to dinner."

So he had played his hand. I didn't know how to respond—after all, I thought I had been giving pastoral care. I wanted to be sure that this was not his vulnerable condition speaking. I told him to think it over and to call me in a week or so. In precisely one week, he called and made the same request: "I'd like to take you to dinner." I had to explain to him that if he was interested in seeing me romantically, I could no longer be his minister. He said, "I've never attended your church—I run on Sunday morning. I've never seen you as my minister." And so it began, this relationship that dazed and confounded me with its arrival.

No, I told him, we could not "go out to dinner": it was way too soon to go out in public; there would be talk, gossip. "Well, maybe could take a walk by the river," he countered. I reminded him that it was February. We wanted to see each other, but we didn't know how. The irony of all this struck me as funny, and I started laughing. I finally broke the impasse by saying, "Why don't you come over to my place, and I'll give you a cooking lesson." (Somehow I knew he had never cooked . . . *never, at all*, and I was right.) We needed to get to know each other, to become not lovers but friends. Was his affection real? Would it hold?

George made himself abundantly clear as we sat on the sofa after dinner. He said, "I know lots of women in this town—I know widows, and I know divorcees, and I'm not interested in them. I'm interested in you." In all my years of being single and dating, no man had ever been so bold, so straightforward. It just isn't done. Dating is a game with parrying, riposte, and yes, painful endings. Here was a man confident of his worth and desirability, clear about his desires, unafraid to take an emotional risk. Compelling beyond words.

In every life there are quintessential moments when your destiny seems clear and indisputable, way beyond agency. You simply acknowledge what you intuitively know to be true. That was the case when I chose Starr King, and again when I answered the call from First Unitarian in Portland. That first evening we were together, George looked at me in wonder, grazed my face with the back of his hand, and said, "You look like a child." He saw the child in the woman, vulnerable and frightened but believing in magic, astounded that he found me lost as I was, and called me home.

Even so, I struggled to accept the love of the only man I ever wanted to marry. Another glitch appeared, knocking hard at my psyche: my old sense that I was not lovable. I imagined that George would be, *should be*, attracted to the kind of woman that most successful men seemed to choose—someone younger, blonder, thinner than myself. Certainly not a difficult, complex woman in her sixties like me.

"Aren't you the beloved?" my spiritual director asked me. I found his words hard to comprehend. My demons were at me again: for some of us, accepting the good is harder than accepting the bad. But George's devotion was finding its way into my heart, tenderly healing some of those early wounds. A year and a half later, we were married in the church I had led for so many years, in an intimate ceremony officiated by Tom Disrud, my partner in ministry.

# 15

## *Too Much, Too Soon*

My cat Bella is a creature of habit. She likes to play with a colored ribbon every evening before bed. She has her favorite foods and turns up her little black nose at anything else. I'm not as rigid as my cat in my predilections, but human creatures, too, find change upsetting, even positive change. Like getting married to the proverbial man of my dreams, after thirty-five years of living alone. Marriage was hugely unsettling to my quiet existence.

After fifteen years, George remains my beloved partner and friend—I have found in marriage many comforts and securities. But no human being lives up to the fantasies one casts upon that person when first falling in love. There were adjustments to be made.

Both of us, for starters, are dominant personalities with strong opinions—about most everything. Generally we agreed, but when we didn't, each of us was quite sure we were right and the other was wrong. George founded his architectural company and had been at it for twenty-five years, and I was the head of a large church—hardly anyone ever told us we could possibly be *wrong* in our thinking. We were both used to speaking *ex cathedra*, not an easy pairing for marriage. There were times when each of us offended the other. There were recriminations, apologies.

I was used to spending long hours alone, reading, contemplating, writing, in absolute silence. I don't play music as I work, nor am I amenable to interruption. As with many men of his generation, George had not developed deep friendships outside the home, so he wanted more attention and interaction than I had expected. He was still working when we married and initially decided to take Mondays off *so we could spend more time together*. This very strong man, this civic leader, this prize-winning architect seemed strangely dependent on me. This closeness was kind of endearing, given the long years I had spent alone. But I found I didn't want that much time with George, or anyone, for that matter. So I was torn—George was never insistent, but I sensed his need for me. I also realized that at our ages, our time on earth was limited, and if the stats played out as usual, I would be alone again one day. I wanted to savor every moment with this man who had been such a late and unexpected blessing in my life.

Then there was the matter of George's grown daughters, who live in Portland. They tried to accept me. They smiled, they hugged, they brought gifts and cards with warm expressions on birthdays and at Christmas. But George and I became involved way too soon after their mom's death for them to adjust easily. Not an unusual response for stepchildren, especially stepdaughters, when their parent chooses a new partner. Their mother had been an extraordinary woman, deeply loving and supportive of them, and they felt her loss keenly. Hoping to become close with them, I had expected too much too soon. Eventually, there was serious conflict, accusations from them that hurt deeply. For several years early in our marriage, George's daughters made their sense of betrayal clear.

I also felt deeply the loss of my house and the neighborhood I loved. George and I both owned large homes when we married. We decided to rid ourselves of many of our accumulated possessions and move to a smaller space where household maintenance would be easier. All so logical. Absolutely the right thing to do, I thought. I hadn't counted on missing the big leaf maple outside my bedroom window, the porch with the wicker rocking chair, the side garden where I planted beans and tomatoes and dahlias, the neighbor children playing in the street. I didn't know how important it was to stop into Peet's Coffee and the Cadillac Café, where the owners knew me. I missed walking the streets in the historic neighborhood each day as I did, admiring the flowering trees and plants, greeting people and their dogs. I had taken this place of beauty and liveliness for granted, and now my home was gone.

The river view from our condo, with its wide, open space and floor-to-ceiling windows, is magnificent, as guests will inevitably remark—but the aesthetic is very different from my craftsman home built at the turn of the century. I had collected antique furniture and paintings from my time in England in the 1970s, but most of it didn't fit in our new home, so I gave many of my treasured pieces—the Regency chest of drawers, the Victorian stained glass window, several Persian rugs—to George's daughters, and sold the rest.

Even though our space is elegant, the feel of the building is institutional, with its long, dimly lit hallways, the brown doors with gold numbers, the elevators, one of which is always out of order. Safe, but not friendly, not open, not like sitting on my front porch in my wicker rocker. More like a hotel room in a strange city. Now I appreciate the beauty and convenience of our condo, but the transition was years in coming. I just didn't count on the sense of dislocation and grief that goes along with such a radical change of living space.

Another major change was the loss of my salary—not having that check come in every month was a little unnerving. George was still working, but despite his assurances, I felt a little guilty about spending money that, after all, I was not making. As time went on, I became an active volunteer, organizing, speaking, writing about climate change. Still, did my work "count," or was it merely make-work, a distraction from my gnawing sense that my efforts were of marginal importance? My discounting of my volunteer efforts didn't come from logic or reason—I did a huge amount of unpaid speaking and writing when I was a minister, but I always thought of that work as part of what any minister would do—after all, the church was supporting me financially so that I could offer my gifts to the community at large.

I think my misgivings were rooted in the voices of a culture that disparages people who are not part of the workforce, voices that say things like, "She's just a housewife." Some people say of those who can't find employment during an economic downturn, "I wonder if they really want to work—I would do anything, flip burgers or whatever, if I couldn't find a job." Or about people from wealthy families, one might hear: "He's never really had to work—he *travels*."

So my leaving the church and then marrying George set off a flurry of changes that my system struggled to assimilate. As I reflect on this time now, I realize the transitions I had experienced were too many, too soon. Both physically and emotionally, I was on overload—this pony reared back and refused to go.

# 16

# *My Body, My Self*

Love and marriage did thankfully solve my loneliness—nonetheless, George's presence in my life, his abiding love, did not prevent my sliding into despair after I left the church. From the outside looking in, I had it all: a place of honor in the community, financial security, the love of a good partner. But still, I felt lost. The pain of not being "in place" soon found its way into my body, pulling at my vitals. I began to have a number of worrisome symptoms—these occurring in a woman who literally never missed a day of work in seventeen years except for a bout of pneumonia.

· · · · · · ·

In the first few years after I leave the church, my sleep suffers. More nights than not, I am haunted by dreams of loss and confusion, sometimes dreams of violence. I wake up shaken, my heart pumping madly, then go back to sleep, only to have the dream continue.

*A man is driving in dry mountainous country. He thinks he knows the way, but he makes a wrong turn, then another, into a road that goes nowhere. It's unbearably hot. He runs out of gas. He gets out of his SUV and looks around. The horizon is empty for miles. He is growing weaker. He doesn't know how to save himself. He dies of heat exhaustion and dehydration. I wonder why he didn't think of some way to signal for help. He could have set the SUV on fire, or even blown it up. Just something. He should have let people know.*

I can't remember names of people, of places. Substitute one word for another. Forget appointments, confuse time—whoops, I'm an hour early, sorry, or maybe a day late, how could I do that? I'm really, really sorry. My psychiatrist tries several drugs, but the side effects leave me shaken and dizzy at best, mentally confused at worst.

My spatial sense has never been a strong suit—now I'm more awkward than ever, bumping into doors and furniture, finding strange bruises on my body: *where did that come from?* Never before have I had a broken bone, but racing to get to a restaurant before closing time and angry at George, I fall down in a parking lot and break my hand. Badly. It is a long healing.

I can no longer tolerate certain scents—I hold my breath while I rush past cosmetic counters in a department store, lest I become lightheaded from the perfume. I can't tolerate glue. Household cleaners make me physically ill—dizzy and foggy-headed. I suffer for many months, consulting one doctor after the next, finally finding some relief by shifting to all-natural products.

Always acutely sensitive to sound, now I feel under attack by our noise-laden culture. In particular, I'm reactive to unexpected loud sounds, including the clanking of dishes, pots and pans. My long-suffering husband puts down his mug of coffee on a stone coaster, and inadvertently, I cry out. A waiter bussing a restaurant table pushes my system into overdrive. I have earplugs in each of my purses for use in movie theaters—absolutely necessary for previews. And, oh—the manufacturers of gasoline-powered leaf blowers should be in the lowest layer of hell.

I can't find a shampoo that won't cause my scalp to break out in red, itchy bumps. After multiple trips to my dermatologist, and many bottles of discarded shampoo and scalp medications, I give up. *Permanent, I guess. Could be worse. Just an allergy to the lack of meaning in my life.*

I think that brain cancer might be the source of the headaches that begin to plague me, headaches that cannot be relieved. My lifelong hypochondria goes into overdrive. *I'm dying, I know I am!* My doctor suggests an MRI, which of course shows nothing.

After preaching with no discomfort for seventeen years, I begin having problems with my voice—with the least little stress, my throat becomes sore, reducing my voice to a whisper. I still do some public speaking, so I consult a voice therapist, who gives me exercises to help me get through speeches or sermons. I become fearful of accepting invitations. I am not unaware of the symbolism of the lost voice of the preacher who has left her pulpit. My dreams fill with failure.

*I have been asked to speak at a school, review a book. I know the expectation is high, for I'm a well-known public speaker. A couple of people are assisting me with the setup. I am late and unprepared. The points I wish to make appear only grudgingly, then disappear, like water curling down a drain. My talk becomes halting and unfocused. I see that I have nothing to give, so I stop. The students file out, my assistants are embarrassed for me. They try to reassure me, saying, "These things happen. Don't worry about it."*

Frightened by pressure in my chest, I'm taken by ambulance to the emergency room with a suspected heart attack. When the ambulance door is opened, sunlight flashes into my face, triggering a grand mal seizure. The diagnosis? Anxiety attack.

One morning I'm sitting on the toilet, and my right arm and hand go numb, my speech becomes garbled. *Obviously a stroke*, I think. I try to tell my husband what is wrong, but the words won't come. Terrified, I'm off to the emergency room again—but it seems I have recovered by the time I arrive. After hours of tests, the doctor says, "I don't know what happened. Could be a TIA."

George and I are in San Francisco, visiting friends—this time the culprit is a racing pulse, which refuses to slow down. Back to the emergency room. Diagnosis: panic attack; remedy: tranquilizers.

The day after I return home from a speaking tour, George hears a loud *thump* and comes into the living room to see me face down, unconscious, in a pool of blood. Back to the emergency room, where I have another grand mal seizure on the examining room table. I have suffered a serious concussion.

The concussion is a warning shot across the bow of a creaking, aging ship carrying way too much cargo. "Just rest," my neurologist says. Not in my repertoire. That would allow my demons to catch up with me.

I constantly feel on edge. Sometimes I take a little Ativan or have a glass of wine to settle down, but I know these remedies are not touching the root problem: I am living in a sea of fear, breathing it through my gills. I have touched down in some primitive place in my psyche, heretofore unacknowledged. No longer can I depend on my elephantine list of duties to distract me from my interior self. *Where, in fact, is the person that had shown up so reliably in my previous life? The woman in charge, the busy one with places to go, things to do?*

# 17

# *Falling into Despair*

Unsurprisingly, I fell into the granddaddy of all depressions. Yes, my old friend had returned with a terrible vengeance. My defenses were not working: without the constraints and distractions of work, repression no longer held me safe, and what therapists call "unfinished business" roared to the front of my psyche.

*I am swimming in shallow water, in a pool crowded with people. I went deep, but when I try to surface, I can't reach the air. I think I'll die.*

Dark moods have dogged me from time to time all my adult life. I come by this honestly, as mental illness runs on both sides of my family. My mother was hospitalized three times with what was probably bipolar disorder. My father was depressed for much of his life, too, and chose alcohol as his medication of choice.

My paternal grandfather, with whom I grew up, was a bright and capable man who rose to become postmaster in his small Louisiana town but then had to retire early because of what the family called "a nervous condition." I remember being terrified as a child when he would have one of his "spells": he would put his head in his hands, rock back and forth, back and forth, and say something like, "I feel like getting that shotgun off the wall and blowing my brains out." And because we did have guns on the wall, as still is common in the South, I thought he might very well carry out his threat. This memory still turns my stomach with fear.

· · · · · ·

Throughout my life, my passion for learning and my love for work were my sure defenses against despair. I stayed in school as long as I could, losing myself in words, in ideas. I was fortunate to find vocations that were right for me, first in teaching, then in ministry, both of which invited more work than could possibly be done. My burden was my salvation.

When I retired, I left the responsibilities that linked me to the people I loved, the reciprocity that gave structure and meaning to my life—the weekly study and sermon preparation, the meetings with staff, the joy of weddings, the profundity of memorial services, the institutional challenges that drove me to pray. Morning meditation, my spiritual grounding, became erratic. Part of the reason I retired was to gain the time to write something other than sermons and reports to the church board. But I doubted the value of my creative writing. Now that I was no longer doing "real work" in the community, why would I covet the spiritual support that I considered absolutely essential to my ministry? *Why would the Holy Spirit care about my writing? My call is done, prayers aren't really needed, because I'm not needed.*

My work at the church had reliably pulled me out of myself and into the world. Even when the bluest of the blue times came, I could respond to the invitations of the larger world. The foggy head would lift, my senses would clear, in spite of the overcast skies and pattering rain of Portland in the winter. Now, though, I stayed stuck in the darkness. I began to think how easy it would be to be dead. How restful.

・・・・・・

*She is distraught, this woman. Too far from her God, from others, from herself. She feels disconnected, as if she's outside, watching herself. She knows her condition is serious because she has been casually thinking of ways she could die without hurting anyone she loves. Stepping in front of a truck or the trolley? That might work—she's always been a little spacey, people would say. But no, she couldn't do that to the driver. She could possibly fake a car accident, but she might fail and end up paraplegic, which would make her even more depressed and less able to kill herself. Besides, she just bought a new Volvo, and Volvos are hard to kill yourself in, they're so safe. And then there's the fact that the car is new—a beautiful deep and shiny red—so what a shame to scratch it, much less crash it.*

*The woman concludes that suicide is a very bad idea. She knows from her time as a minister that relatives and friends suffer deeply and at great length when someone they love kills themselves. She herself had a friend who died after swallowing a whole bottle of tranquilizers. Though the death occurred fifteen years ago, the woman still feels a wave of sadness with the memory. She wishes fervently that her friend was alive still. Wishes she had been there to stop her friend. "Don't take the pills! Don't you see that so many of us love you?" Of course, that's not the point with depression. It's the unremitting pain, the desolation of separation, the failure of hope to whisper that a better day will come.*

*The woman knows she herself would never bring this kind of grief to her husband, her sons. And what about her former congregants? Over and over again, she asked them to choose life. So she chooses an alternative plan: go to her psychiatrist and get an antidepressant. She has taken them off and on her whole adult life. So here we go again, she thinks. Damn. Hope the little white pills work.*

*The writer's mood changes. She wants to eat again, see movies. She speaks to people in the elevator in her condo and smiles, makes one of those ubiquitous comments about the weather, like "enjoying the sun?" She's reasonably content again (i.e., at least she's not considering suicide anymore) and eventually understands that she wants to write another book, maybe a book about death, which after all has become her obsession. Or maybe one about retirement, which was a kind of death for her. Maybe she could help others, help herself. She no longer knows what her life is about. She needs to figure that out.*

# III

# Searching

# 18

## *Looking for Answers*

On the first day after I left the church, I sat down at my computer to see what words might come forth. What was I curious about, what did I want to explore? Spontaneously, I started writing a long essay on death, which went through many drafts in the months to come. I loved writing this essay, loved writing it more than I ever loved writing anything—the subject was so absolutely, terrifyingly relevant. That old black raven perched on my shoulder that fateful day and never really left.

I began to see that I was experiencing retirement as *a kind of death*—not just the end of a phase of life but a portent of more and more endings, until I would *be* no more. Upon leaving work, many retirees begin to sense their mortality as never before. *Impermanence, that difficult and omnipresent law of the universe.*

So how should I move forward now that the fear of death had taken root in my gut? I decided to do what I always do to figure out stuff—stuff like how to cook a turkey or how far is it from here to Poughkeepsie: I did research. I perused studies by physicians and social scientists. Articles, books, news features. I had conversations with individuals who were at different stages of retirement. *What were the circumstances of your leaving work was it your choice? What happened to your friendships at the office? How do you feel about no longer commanding a salary? How do you structure your time, without the strictures that work gave? Do you experience depression?*

Most of the self-help literature I read was irritating or actually insulting. The scenarios sounded unappealing, depressing. Lots of empty generalizations, slogans about retirement "plans" and "new life." Cute names, like "re-firement." Stats about money and best places to live. My soul was hurting, and I was being flooded with practical advice about getting new hobbies and investing my nest egg. I was being given cheerleaders, and I needed a wise coach. I needed to go deeper.

I found it difficult to get candid statements from many of the recent retirees I spoke with. Most people would begin our conversation smiling and saying how great retirement is, talking about newfound freedom, travel. I gently pushed to see what was beneath their reluctance to reveal negative feelings. I asked about loneliness and longing. I asked about fear. I asked about hope, or the lack thereof. When I brought up questions about "the meaning of your life," some balked, hesitated, even grew weepy.

Not to say everyone is reluctant to leave work, though. Some retirees seem to have little angst, and seem to simply relish the freedom. Typically, these individuals had never been enamored of their work. Charlene, who retired at sixty-nine after spending long years as a development director, was elated upon leaving her position. She had studied ancient Greek theater and renaissance art in college, but these disciplines had not prepared her to make a living, so she fell completely by accident into work as a fundraiser. "It is very easy to be hired in development, but not easy to be happy," she said. "Your value as an employee comes down to the amount of money you raise." She said that now she has a chance to become thoroughly herself. She does the reading she'd never had time for, and has joined the board of a non-profit seeking to re-open an inpatient hospice.

I found Charlene's work history sad, but it's the story of many people who work at a job they don't enjoy, driven by necessity rather than inclination. Some chose a profession that promised a good living, as when a father influences a son to take over the family business. I've known lawyers who hated their work—in fact, two students out of twelve in my seminary class were disaffected lawyers. A trader on Wall Street, flush with money, once told me, "You have to run with the sharks." These individuals will have adjustments to make when they leave their jobs, but their chief feeling is one of relief—they will likely not miss work.

The majority of retirees I spoke with are traversing a more or less predictable path: (1) initially, glad to be free from the constraints of paid employment; (2)

feeling lost, with no clear direction and too much time on their hands; (3) grieving the loss of companionship and the loss of identity, as well as awakening to the reality of their mortality; (4) exploring various alternatives, trying some on for size, learning when to say yes, when to say no; (5) eventually arriving at a new identity, a place of relative peace and satisfaction.

But for the 30 percent of working people who had found their work lives highly fulfilling, as I did—retirement is often devastating. The center is gone. Identity is gone. They are confronted with the most profound questions of being. For people like us, the transition requires a period of serious reflection and substantial adjustment.

As I continued to look for answers, I discovered patterns. Some workers commonly have a tougher time: those who leave work not by choice, but because they are laid off; men who heavily identify with their work—and are less likely than women to ask for help; soldiers who cannot adjust to life without the structure of the military and the close relationships they formed there; athletes who age out of their professions. And then there are leaders, like myself, who have their own particular challenges.

# 19

# *Involuntary Job Loss*

For some people, work stops abruptly. If your work is your reason for being, leaving in this manner catapults you into a vast and painful emptiness. One day you are playing in the orchestra, or managing the office, or designing the building, or teaching your students, and the next day you are in free fall. You were full of plans and possibility, connected with others in common purpose. *I work, therefore I am.* You could go on forever, you think, building, healing, advising, creating—but through no fault of your own, your story has come to a screeching halt. I wasn't fired, of course, but because of the retirement ethic of my denomination, I was there fully, heartfully, one day, and then completely absent the next. The experience was brutal and disorienting.

With the downturn in the economy in 2008, many men—often those in blue collar jobs—were "retired" against their will, and some were not able to find work again after years of trying. The terminology that goes along with being laid off is harsh: we say a person has been "dismissed," "sacked," "terminated." I talked with one man who was devastated when his company was downsized—he, along with a number of others, were told with no warning that their jobs were gone. They were ordered to gather their personal items in a cardboard box and leave the office immediately. Such an approach is far from rare in company culture.

Maybe the technology is changing, and you can't keep up, so you are let go to make way for the young, the clever. Maybe the company has been sold and is being reorganized, so you're given the option of an early retirement. The money looks good, and logic tells you, "Hey, why not?" A lawyer friend of mine found that his specialty at the firm had become obsolete, so even though he was a partner, he was voted out and given a year's severance. For him, a disastrous turn of events. He tried to find work as a consultant but failed. Formerly president of Portland's City Club, he started a new civic group focusing on urban issues, inviting friends and former colleagues to a series of meetings, but he couldn't stir up interest. His health—mental and physical—went into a steep decline. For a while, he was even homeless.

For some individuals, the pain of being laid off is compounded by other losses. A journalist friend, Alice, was let go after eighteen years of writing for a newspaper when her beat, religion, was dropped. That same year, her spouse died suddenly, and she found herself bewildered and deeply depressed. Who was she without her job and without the man who was her closest friend and companion? After about two years, she began writing again, eventually placing a book with a leading religious publisher—but she still sometimes tears up when she remembers the time her world fell apart.

Another individual I know lost his communications job at a university just as his wife was telling him she wanted a divorce. His only child went off to college. Then his dog died. For a while, he had trouble retrieving the right words in ordinary conversation. He drifted for many months, with little to anchor him. Eventually, he built a consulting practice.

There has not been sufficient study on the effects of retirement on health and well-being to generalize about this. However, involuntary job loss has been studied in some detail. One study links involuntary job loss with increased alcohol consumption. The Health and Retirement Study by the University of Michigan, the most comprehensive national survey thus far, showed devastating effects of involuntary job loss on both physical function and mental health. The authors posit a causal relationship between job loss and morbidity. I totally understand how this could be the case: *I give, therefore I am.*

# 20

# *Males Are More Vulnerable*

A psychiatrist said to me in a casual conversation, "I can't begin to tell you how many men become depressed after they retire." Males, more than females, find their identity in work. Men are particularly vulnerable to loss of all kinds, says Alan Berman, PhD, who is executive director of the American Association of Suicidology in Washington, D.C. Some men, says Berman, in deference to work, have neglected relationships with family and friends and so do not have deep human connections to turn to when they retire. Compounding that problem is the well-known reluctance of many males to share their feelings of loneliness and sadness, afraid of being thought weak.

Men of a certain age—self-esteem gone, their role as provider done—may no longer want to live. Some of the current increase in mortality for men is undoubtedly due to opioid addiction, a no-win solution for those who fall into despair, but between 2001 and 2021, the national suicide rate increased by one-third, with males four times more likely than females to kill themselves. Researchers have been dumbfounded by the 28 percent increase in the number of men aged thirty-five to sixty-four who commit suicide. Between ages sixty-five and eighty-five, the suicide rate for men actually doubles. Men are most likely to kill themselves at two times in their life: at the death of a spouse and at the time of retirement.

Leaving certain male-oriented professions is particularly problematic—jobs like soldiering, for example. The soldier is awake, alive, as in no other place, no other time. They have a command protocol, and they may give up their life to save another, or for the greater good. Meaning is not elusive. When soldiers return to civilian life, they may find the pursuits of others—spouse, friends, family—shallow, inconsequential. And many, of course, suffer from PTSD. Veterans have a 57 percent higher risk of suicide than those who haven't served.

Similarly, police officers are encouraged to see themselves as part of a family. Then one day, they find themselves with no badge, no uniform, no identity. Too many of them go into retirement with years of unresolved emotional issues, then feel alone, without the "family" that held them in spite of the burdens and dangers of their work. Emotional trauma is a part of the working life of a police officer, and it exacts a price—all too often, officers lose relationships, turn to alcohol or drugs. The average police officer dies within five years after retirement and has a life expectancy of twelve years less than that of other people.

In today's cultural climate of protests against police brutality, police officers have been retiring in record numbers. They no longer feel respected as public servants, and many have suffered abuse themselves, with protesters throwing rocks and bottles at them. Scores have been injured in Portland, over 2,000 nationwide. I know of one Portland officer who was harassed for weeks, his house egged, the windows broken. He ended up not only quitting his job but leaving Portland. Another officer here in Portland developed PTSD and is afraid to leave his home. Fear is not an unrealistic response: In 2023, 136 federal, state and local law enforcement officers died in the line of duty, a 39 percent decrease from 2022. Officials speculate that advances in medical treatment and training account for the decrease in fatalities.

I was not a soldier or a police officer, but what I have in common with them is the fierce bonding I had with those in my community. Now, fourteen years later, I still feel pangs of grief when I hear of a new death in the congregation. I remember them as they were, their very particular way of standing, the sound of their voice. I wasn't just offering professional services, I had allowed my heart to open to these individuals.

Just today, I cut out of the *Oregonian* an obituary of Mary Bothwell, who died at ninety-eight. It was in her charming cottage in Eastmoreland where

I first met with the search committee from First Unitarian and told them, prophetically, that I believed I was called to be their minister.

Several weeks ago, I gave a sermon at a UU church in Salem, Oregon, and noticed a familiar face in the receiving line at the end of the service. He didn't acknowledge me, but as he passed through, I realized that he was a former congregant. "Paul!" I called out to him as he headed out the door. He turned, came closer. He looked forlorn. I noticed food stains on his shirt. I said, "Paul, how are you?"

"My wife died," he said, "and I'm having a hard time." One of the privileges of ministry is the raw emotional honesty that people are willing to share. Our touching in was brief, and all the moment allowed was my presence and a warm hug. But this gesture carried power, I knew. I'll let the minister of the church know of his distress, and more help will be forthcoming.

Recently I ran into a woman in the parking lot of the Old Spaghetti Factory, one of many in my large congregation whose names I never learned. She called out to me over the expanse of concrete, "Marilyn, I still hear your words in my head!" I am comforted by the staying power of words, hers and mine. I write, claiming a share in the future, knowing the deathless power of words. *Make them strong, make them loving.*

# 21

# *Some Age Out*

Some people simply age out of their profession.

Professional athletes face retirement earlier than most of us. Even the most skilled, the most talented, have to ask, "What next?" They leave the only work they have known, work they have been deeply committed to from their youth. I just heard an interview with soccer star Megan Rapinoe, who said something like, "Retiring at thirty-seven? That's the subject for a whole other interview!"

Extensive interviews were done in 2015 with twenty-five football players who were first-round picks in the 1990 draft. Many were ill-equipped for life away from football. They spoke of difficulty coping with the loss of their positions, as well as the routine provided by the sport. Some lacked marketable skills. Lingering injuries contributed to their physical problems, and of course we now know that the negative effect of concussions in football is virtually universal. In the first years after they quit playing, many lost energy and became depressed. These athletes experienced earlier and in a more extreme way what many workers experience as they grow older and are no longer able to perform at a job that gave their lives meaning and purpose.

Some athletes attempt a comeback and succeed, like Olympic swimmer Michael Phelps, the most decorated Olympian in history. Phelps struggled when he left competitive swimming after winning four gold and two silver medals at the 2012 London Olympics. He felt lost without the training and the schedules that structured his life. His weight went from 187 to nearly 230 pounds. In an interview with Bob Costas, Phelps said that he still "remembers the days locked in my room, not wanting to talk to anybody, not wanting to see anybody, not really wanting to live." Phelps did come back, triumphant, winning five golds and one silver in 2016 in Rio de Janeiro. And eventually he found his way through to a satisfying retirement. He became an ambassador for the Special Olympics, and he created the Michael Phelps Foundation, focusing on helping young people follow their dreams. He is married and has three young children.

Clyde Drexler was an All-Star basketball player with the Portland Trail Blazers. A friend of mine who did not follow basketball happened to have her car break down in front of Drexler's home in Dunthorpe, a wealthy area of town. She rang his doorbell and asked for help, which he kindly tendered. While she was waiting for AAA, she began chatting with Drexler, not having any idea that he was a famous basketball star—but she did recognize that he was very, very tall. "So what do you do?" she asked.

Drexler said, "I play basketball."

Concerned, she responded, "But what will you do when you can no longer play basketball?"

Drexler answered, "Any damn thing I want to." True, but still, he had to find his way to a new identity. Drexler went on to be a coach and a TV personality and commentator.

Legendary dancer Martha Graham once said, "A dancer dies twice—once when they stop dancing, and this death is the more painful." Wendy Whelan, A dancer with the New York City Ballet, was called in 2012 in The *New York Times* "America's greatest contemporary ballerina." But in 2011, at forty-four, her age was already catching up with her: ballet master-in-chief Peter Martins called her into his office and told her she wouldn't be dancing the Sugarplum Fairy in *The Nutcracker* anymore. She was shocked—she had danced the role for twenty-two years, half her life. He added, "I want you to only look [your] best on stage. And I don't think this makes you look your best."

Then in the fall of 2012, she slipped and injured her hamstring. She kept trying to dance, but she was feeling pain in her hip. An exam showed that she had a labral tear. She was done—she had to watch much younger dancers take her roles at the NYCB. She thought, *I never had a baby. I never took the time away*. She had given all her youth to ballet, which requires extraordinary devotion to a career that is relatively brief. Largely unprepared, she was faced with making a new life for herself.

Whelan's story ends well, though. She decided to focus on contemporary dance, leaving her ballet company in 2014, after thirty years. She went on to teach, becoming an artist-in-residence at Barnard College, and then in 2019 was named Associate Artistic Director of NYCB. It's possible to turn interests, skills, and experience into a satisfying new life, but to do so, a retiree must be intentional—must learn and reflect and experiment and decide.

# 22

# *Some Continue to Work*

Many workers do not have the luxury of retiring—*ever*, because they have been unable to save enough money to meet their basic needs in retirement. Even as they deal with the constraints of aging, they have to continue working to stay afloat. Consider the demographics: nearly half of households headed by someone fifty-five or older have no retirement savings at all. Of those sixty-five to seventy-four, the median savings is $200,000. Almost 70 percent of elders are expected to need extended services at some point, but one in four seniors are trying to get by on Social Security alone, with an average benefit of $1,913 a month.

The Academy Award-winning film *Nomad* shows in heartbreaking detail the lives of wandering workers, mostly aged and infirm, who travel in vans of varying sizes and condition to whatever seasonal work they can find. Many of the characters in the film are not professional actors, but actual nomads, who add great pathos and authenticity to this work of fiction.

Some older workers may not be in dire need, but they enjoy working, or they can use the extra money. They often segue into some other kind of work, paid or volunteer, as they leave their careers. The Sloan Center on Aging and Work, in its report "Working in Retirement: a 21st Century Phenomenon," stated that 75 percent of workers expect to work in some capacity after they retire.

As some people age, they may shift the emphasis of their work life to something that feels more feasible. Some employers are able to offer a gradual leave-taking, reducing hours and levels of responsibility, easing the shift into retirement. Ilana Benet left her position as a labor and delivery nurse at age sixty, but it soon hit her: "I miss the babies!" And her employer missed her. Within a few weeks, Ilana was back on the maternity ward, working as a freelancer two days a week at $60 an hour, pay she received in addition to her pension. Kathleen Christensen, who funds research on aging and the American labor market, points out, "In a tight labor market, firms find recent retirees increasingly attractive. Their skills are up-to-date, they possess critical institutional knowledge, and they can mentor younger workers."

A doctor friend of mine says that when he retires, he's going to walk his dog in the woods. I'm thinking . . . *and*? I recently learned that he has begun filling in for doctors on vacation. Another doctor, John V. Siebel, at sixty-four had become burdened by the heavy load of administrative tasks that modern medicine requires. He quit his busy practice and now he works three months out of the year in remote areas where a medical employment agency books him. Siebel sees patients during the week and on weekends explores the wilderness.

If you're self-employed like my friend Pat, an investment advisor, you can choose how much work you want to take on—Pat has retained a few clients and let the rest go. Thomas Murphy, a construction engineer in Atlanta who worked for United Parcel Service, accepted a generous early retirement package at age fifty. At first he and his wife traveled, then they started a small construction firm that trains disadvantaged young people.

Upon leaving a career, retirees may ask the question, "How do I give of myself, of the store of knowledge, wisdom, and experience I have gradually, painstakingly built during a lifetime of meaningful work?" Some retirees may begin teaching or consulting, drawing on their many years of experience. A basketball player becomes a coach. A carpenter trains younger workers. The immensely talented Luciano Pavarotti, the best-known opera singer of his generation, continued to sing as he aged. His voice failed to live up to the greatness of his early career, but he began teaching master classes. His greatest joy late in life was the foundation he established, which encourages young opera singers and sponsors events all over the world.

Some fortunate people simply love their work and say, "I'll never retire!" A therapist I know recently decided to close her practice—but she was clear that the word *retire* was meaningless to her. She said, with a good deal of passion and conviction, that she's never going to stop working. She is determined to find new avenues of creating and giving.

Financial reasons play a role, people report, but most continue to work because they enjoy it and want to remain active and involved. Many of these are high achievers who simply can't give up the satisfaction of working. Elizabeth Olson recounts the story of a "driven achiever," Ronald E. Steward, who left a thirty-year career at fifty-three, only to start a private equity investment firm. Another opportunity came up, and he decided to open a hamburger restaurant with a young man he had mentored. Olson quotes Steward as saying, "Waking up and doing something you want to do sort of gets in your DNA. I never felt comfortable chilling out."

A friend of mine, Charlie, had been working at Harvard with social justice change agents around the world. Initially, he said he was planning to retire, move to Colorado, and live in an idyllic little town set at the foot of the Rockies. Ah, dreams! He bought a house and fixed it up, but when that project was done, he became instantly bored. He decided to move to Berkeley, where his son is attending college and where Charlie has already taken a full-time job as a college administrator. He is seventy-two years old and still has infectious energy—I can't imagine that he'll ever want to stop working.

I just saw the racehorse Seize the Day win the Preakness—the trainer was 88-year-old D. Wayne Lukas, for whom this was the seventh Preakness win. A journalist asked him just after the race, "How do you feel about all these other trainers coming up and congratulating you?" Lukas answered with a smile, "They're probably hoping I'll go away, but I'm not going to."

We see performers who refuse to stop. Marian McPartland, a well-known jazz pianist and host of the National Public Radio (NPR) show "Piano Jazz," died at the age of ninety-five, "of natural causes," the obituary stated. Yes, death is so very natural—but retirement is not, at least for some of us. When McPartland was eighty-nine, she said in an interview with the Associated Press, "Retire? Why retire? I've got a job, I'm making money, I like what I do. I think I'll jump out of a cake, or something." Like a chorus girl in a musical extravaganza? Like a stripper at a bachelor party? I think she may have meant *I'm still alive, still female, still sensual, still, for God's sake, celebrating. Stop being me and doing what I do? Why would I do that?*

Tony Bennett didn't slow down until he was ninety-four and diagnosed with Alzheimer's disease. Lady Gaga honored Bennett at the Grammys in 2022, singing the tracks "Love for Sale," Bennett's final project. And then there is the indomitable Willie Nelson. Nelson celebrated his ninetieth birthday in April of 2023 by doing two concerts at the Hollywood Bowl—and now he's "on the road again," touring. Bob Dylan, eighty-three, is currently touring the country and has twenty-two upcoming concerts.

Many writers, artists, and teachers continue to work their whole life long. William Stafford, US Poet Laureate in 1970, was doing some of his most memorable work when he died in 1993 at the age of seventy-nine. Designer Giorgio Armani, ninety years of age, is presently working on multiple collections. Jane Goodall, also ninety, travels widely, urging us to save our earth and its creatures. She reports that she has spent only five nights at home since the middle of January 2024.

Those who pursue post-retirement work have better mental and physical health than those who retire fully, studies say. But as age and illness arrive, many will find that their work lives are increasingly constrained. The poet Donald Hall reached a place in his eighties where, as he said, "poems aren't coming anymore," and so he turned to prose. Even as he struggled physically and mentally, he continued writing, and writing well. He left us with several moving articles and two books on his own aging process.

Elaine Stritch, the singer and stage performer, died at eighty-nine in 2014, following the release of a documentary film, *Elaine Stritch: Shoot Me*, about her life and work. Stritch had been in show business for seventy years. The film asks a question that many of us ask after leaving a profession we love: without doing what I do, who am I? Stritch admits that the love she receives from her audiences is essential for her. In a difficult-to-watch sequence, she is shown doing her last cabaret show, sharing with her audience her struggle to remember song lyrics. Still, I left the theater feeling inspired—she clearly ended her days "raging against the dying of the light."

# 23

# *Work Ethic in My Family*

Seven years after retirement, I was still struggling to find a way forward. My research was interesting and passably helpful, but ultimately all my searching did not satisfy my soul's sickness. Who was I, now that my red ministerial robe was encased in a plastic bag?

Every retirement experience is unique, for every retirement emerges from a life narrative. What forces, natural and environmental, shaped us? How did our family of origin deal with work? What themes appear over and over? Where are the sources of power, the touchstones of safety? What demands our allegiance? And most important, what have we told ourselves about who we are? We do not spring up de novo, any of us. We flower, or fail to flower, from seeds planted long, long ago.

I come from an extended family of people who all worked, and worked hard—my attitudes and assumptions about work were first formulated there. And no doubt, I carried these kinfolk and their behaviors forward into my own life, however unconsciously. Not a remarkable insight, but something that never had occurred to me. We grow up with what *is*, and we all too often simply accept these values without question.

From age nine, I lived, along with my father and my younger brother and sister, in the home of my paternal grandparents. My grandparents had gone through the Great Depression and knew what it meant to have only one egg in the house. It went to the father, of course. My grandmother's main relationship was not with her husband or even with her children, but with God, and her fealty afforded her a sacred bond that got her through a lifetime with a dominating husband, through years of want, through the work that came with raising seven children of her own and partially raising six more, as fractures in the extended family demanded. She made clothes for those children on an old Singer sewing machine with a foot pedal. She took in boarders. She even cut her long tresses to sell for hairpieces, I am told.

By the time we arrived in the household, my grandmother was elderly. She padded around the house in her thin voile dress, read her Bible in her big blue easy chair, and kept the flowers blooming in the yard. She also baked and fried and stewed, and the vegetables and fruits we couldn't eat in the summer—peaches, peas, tomatoes, figs—she canned for winter days. And she prayed. Always she prayed. Each night before bed, I knelt and prayed with her. She would start with the Lord's Prayer, moving on to pray for her seven children, each by name, then for the president of the United States, and finally for "people all the world over" who were in pain or sorrow. Daddy called her "Mama," and we children called her "Granny." Big Papa always said he married her because she was the prettiest girl in the county. Her given name was Gertrude. Gertrude Virginia Honeycutt. It's written in the family Bible.

In his younger days, my grandfather had served as the town postmaster, but I knew him only as Big Papa, an elderly man with a full head of blond hair, a roman nose, and an excess of moral rectitude. Papa raised most of the food we ate in his half-acre plot: tomatoes, green beans, black-eyed peas, butter beans, potatoes, turnip greens, cantaloupe, onions, okra. We had a hen house, a cage for rabbits. Each spring, he would hire out a mule and a plow, and wearing a string T-shirt and an explorer's hat, he would run the earth into rows for planting, the sweat dripping off his face and body. Big Papa's Victorian moralism set the standard in our home, and he felt that being idle was the greatest sin of all. On Saturday mornings, when we three kids were hoping to sleep late, he would rouse us at 8:00 a.m.: "A birdie with a yellow bill hopped upon my windowsill, cocked his shining eye and said, 'Aren't you ashamed, you sleepy head.'" No layabouts allowed.

We lived in an atmosphere of scarcity. The woodwork was never repainted, the wallpaper grew tired and began to peel off the wall. My father was the quintessential lovable rogue who escaped to women and drink. He knew how to have fun, but his brand of fun seemed morally unacceptable, even dangerous. From time to time, Papa had to bail him out of jail for drunk driving.

In fact, all fun was of questionable merit in our household. We did not have music, nor puzzles, nor games—well, except dominos. Big Papa walked to the courthouse every weekday, dressed in his vest with the gold watch pocket, and played dominos with his cronies. Or he roped in my grandmother and played on the front porch. I can still smell the talcum powder that allowed the slick movement of the dominos. Cards, on the other hand, were considered immoral, possibly because Daddy gambled away a good deal of his salary. We were allowed to watch television at night and regularly saw shows like "Hit Parade" and "Gunsmoke." Those came only after we gathered around the radio to hear Brother J. Harold Smith, the evangelist out of Del Rio, Texas, with his message of sin and salvation. Vacations? A foreign concept. Virtue was found in work. Always.

Although neither of my parents graduated from high school, both closely identified with their work. My mother, Marion, started her career at age fourteen as a dancer and traveled in shows all over the United States. She reveled in the glamour, the adventure, the laughter, the men. Then the economy collapsed, and the dancing stopped. She put away her costumes and began selling Goody hair curlers. She made her customers feel beautiful and special, and more importantly, she made them laugh in those hard times. She met my father in Washington, D.C., where he had found work as a cook and waiter in a German restaurant. Theirs was a love match, but the city girl and the country boy couldn't make a life together.

After my father took us children from her, she spent the rest of her work life as a domestic, cooking and cleaning for wealthy Cincinnatians. During her last decade, she cooked for a group of six priests in a Cincinnati diocese. Devoted Catholic that she was, she took great pleasure in serving the priests—cocktails at 5:00 p.m., dinner at 6:00, on the dot. They became a family, these six clerics and my mother. When she died, they prepared a funeral high mass to honor her, filled with anecdotes about "their Marion." No negative thinking from her, the priest recalled: "Not my cup of tea," he quoted her as saying.

My father was an oil field worker in Louisiana—he "stabbed pipe" and so was called when a well came in. He worked in the top of the derrick, typically

70 to 100 feet tall, in all kinds of weather—rain, sleet, burning sun—guiding the pipe into the ground. It was dangerous work, but it paid well. In the bottom of his chest of drawers lay hidden a deerskin pouch containing a rabbit's foot, a good luck charm his beloved Grandma Honeycutt had given him as a child. He grew teary whenever he spoke of her. There he tucked away the money that sent each of his three children to college.

When he was off work, Daddy lay in bed in his boxer shorts in the back bedroom shaded by the black walnut tree, smoking Picayune cigarettes and reading detective magazines. Becoming restless after a time, he would take off in his big blue-green Olds 88 to see his girlfriend in another town. There were always girlfriends—my father was handsome and dark, like Johnny Cash. And he drank. Since we lived in a dry parish, he got his whiskey wherever he could, generally from Pee Wee's filling station, catty-corner from First Baptist Church. Only work kept him sober, tamped down his shame and self-remorse. Strange—everybody loved my father, but he couldn't love himself. He worked until he couldn't work, when alcohol dementia put him in the state hospital.

·······

Even when I became a minister with a good salary, it never occurred to me to take time off for rest and renewal. One day a couple of women congregants invited me to go with them to Oaxaca. Oaxaca, *Mexico*? I couldn't think of a reason to refuse—and that trip became my first vacation. After eight years of ministry, I took a long sabbatical—I went first to Cuba, then to Bali. I told the congregation, "I want to go where my assumptions will be challenged." That is, to learn. Not for pleasure, you understand—though during these trips I began to see the joys of visiting interesting and faraway places.

Another reason for placing work at the center of my life was that I didn't have any backup—there would be no inheritance, no bailouts. My father left only enough social security money to bury him. My mother left an opal ring for my sister, and for me, a cheap watch on a neck chain. After her death, we found in her small apartment some cookware, blackened with age and use, and some ragged embroidered doilies. She was buried in a housedress. Whatever I made of myself wouldn't rest on resources from my family. Knowing that will light a fire under a person.

My grandparents didn't have money, but they owned their home and ate from the garden, so they got by with Big Papa's social security check. Each Christmas, they gave each of us three children an orange and a silver dollar. What I did receive as bequests, though, came from them—nothing material, but two possessions which ultimately became touchstones for me: my grandmother's Bible, the pages well-worn from turning, and my grandfather's antique pencil sharpener. They had seven children and many, many grandchildren—so it's a mystery to me still why I ended up with these two items. I had no inkling where time and fate would take me, but the gifts were prescient: I became a minister and a writer.

# 24

# *Taking Care of Business*

I wonder about the less-than-conscious motivation for my unrelenting fixation on work. I'm still compelled to *produce*. Maybe writing a book—or maybe just doing the laundry. Just *doing*. What led that child to become an adult who rested her worthiness in work? What was I trying to make right, to redeem?

My family of origin was fractured. In the South, we have this notion about family, about those who come from a "good family" and others who come from "bad blood." I grew up ashamed. Ashamed of a father who came home from time to time staggering drunk and who hung out with violent men. Daddy's best friend, J. P. Peterson, ended up with his body on the street, surrounded by a white chalk mark. Somebody in the family had to balance out Daddy's sins, after all—why not me, the eldest child?

Ashamed that I had no mother—I was the only child I knew whose parents were divorced. Ashamed that roaches ran rampant in the kitchen at night. I responded the way most children do when adults fail them: I came to believe I was somehow at fault—that I had some kind of built-in, inherent flaw that must be atoned for. It followed, as the day follows the night, that *work* and *virtue* became my twin obsessions.

The summer we left Mother, when I turned ten, I became a grown-up. Except for a few fragile images, my years with my mother were wiped from memory. Recently, my brother told me that our mother actually came to Louisiana for a visit when I was in the seventh grade. He said she and our father quarreled, and Mother left after a couple of days. I have no recollection of that visit whatsoever. When truth is unbearable, we simply shut it out.

Even as a child, I took it upon myself to restore order, to repair the brokenness. I could always push through, take care of business. *I hear my grandmother call out in the night, guttural sounds, not words. Soon everyone is up—Big Papa and Donna and Jim. Daddy isn't home. What to do but call Dr. Tatum. I know he will come, doctors always come. I'm only twelve, the directory is shaking in my hand, but I find the number, make the call. I make it because nobody else is capable of making it.*

How was I supposed to *relax? Play?* In my new life in Louisiana, I watched over my little brother and sister, tried to please my aging grandparents, and, in fact, became the moral voice that my father was unable to provide: my assigned role in the family system.

・・・・・・

As an adolescent, I was tall, slump-shouldered, chronically sad. During all of high school, I carried around in my billfold a saying I'd cut from some magazine or newspaper: "We all have to play the cards we were dealt, so why expect a reshuffle?" I went to church three times a week—Sunday morning, Sunday evening, and Wednesday night choir practice and prayer meeting. I wasn't popular, I was pious. How else could I have gotten elected "Best Christian" at First Baptist my senior year? That same year I was elected "Most Intelligent" at school, and I won a national title, "Miss Betty Crocker Homemaker of Tomorrow." Laid before me were the dominant goals of my life: I would be good, I would achieve, and I would marry and have a home of my own. If I could be good enough, could achieve enough, then I would earn the right to breathe air and take up space on the earth. And the most elusive, yet most coveted goal of all: I just might one day be the chosen one, the one who was loved.

It was not, though, just guilt and self-recrimination that fueled my character development. From the time I was quite young, I saw my life as a sacred trust, the ground beneath my existence. Not that I would have used these words—I simply had this sense as far back as I can remember. It was my job to live up to that trust, to show myself well in all matters—in my schoolwork as well as in my character. Where did this feeling come from—this sense that I must be not just good, but worthy? Perhaps from the women in my life, who modeled both faith and virtue. First my mother, then my grandmother, also Aunt Mellie, my father's sister, with whom I lived during the fifth grade.

Not long ago, I rediscovered two five-year diaries that I kept during the years I lived in Homer with my grandparents. There I recorded the little pleasures of everyday living: digging with my hands for potatoes in the rich soil of our garden; collecting warm brown eggs from the nests of our hens; making my good dog Rusty howl when I practiced my coronet; playing guard on the girls' basketball team; swimming in the Olympic-size pool in the heat of the Louisiana summer; standing in a circle with the youth group at First Baptist and singing "Kum ba yah"; going to band camp at Caney Lake; cutting into the first watermelon of the summer, huge and running with juice, on my July birthday; spending the night with the widow next door, hearing her squeal over Liberace: I recorded all this and so much more. Finding these simple writings shifted my understanding about those years. Yes, I was a lost child with no mother, all that hurt was real . . . and yet, like any young person, I had my joys, my adventures. School and church and a whole slew of neighbors were the stabilizing forces in my life. Thinking back, I realize that not a single family ever moved from our neighborhood. I was part of a larger community that held me in its keeping, and for that I remain so very grateful.

As an adult, I spent multiple years in psychotherapy with some very fine practitioners—and I tried myself out in the world, and did well. So I mostly left behind the notion that I was broken beyond repair. But the impulse to make all things right is still with me. And the confidence that I can do whatever needs to be done. The mother lion picks up her cub in her mouth and moves it to safe ground. Never mind its chances of reaching adulthood are maybe one in two—she knows what her task is, and she's not going to be deterred from it. That's me, always has been, as long as I remember. Pick up the cub. Just pick up the cub.

Even as a child—at least after we left Mother—I never had much imagination for play. A few years ago, two young girls rang my doorbell here in Portland. When I saw their smiling faces, their eyes full of wonder and anticipation, I thought, "I used to be a girl, but not like these girls." They told me, tripping over each other's words, "We're selling raffle tickets for our school—you could win a trip to Disneyland!"

Before I caught myself, I said, "Vacation from hell."

# 25

# *Who Are My People Now?*

The difficulty of the transition out of work is rarely articulated and therefore often goes unacknowledged—cut off from tribe and community, retirees may well become quietly desolate. People who are still working ask, "How's retirement?" They're still pushing through their workdays, perhaps, and so may see you as lucky to be free of all that. How can you tell someone that you're bereft, that you've begun to question who you are and why you're even living? So you skirt your deepest truth: "Just great!" you say. And smile.

Work offers a natural setting for daily interactions, which are often casual and at other times, actually profound—at least for those still working in person. Even a job that we're not particularly fond of has its social benefits, for as we begin our workday, we fall into relationship. We may perhaps share only a greeting, but that simple social convention brings order and meaning to our day. We share thoughts, judgments about tasks at hand. We may also speak of personal matters. We make ourselves known, and others reciprocate, not by content alone, but by tone of voice, by every careless glance. Friendly contact, maybe camaraderie, comes with the territory. We take our coworkers for granted until they're gone, as we do with so many of those who make up the fabric of our lives.

We may not get along with every single person, but we're contributing to a common endeavor, and in healthful places of work, our efforts are honored and appreciated. We are accountable to others and we produce something or other, whether it's a lesson plan or a proposal or a manuscript or an object or an invention. We may have clients or patients that we are particularly fond of.

Even if our contact is on a superficial level, we are in *relationship*. We are part of a larger whole, and for tribal creatures like ourselves, that counts for a lot.

Not only must we structure our time in retirement—the forty or more hours we spent working each week—but we have to search out new companions, as well. We often find that we have little in common with our old workmates. They may not even welcome us as friends, as Diana, an outstanding physician, found. She interrupted her medical practice to stay at home with her children, but when she reached out, suggesting lunch or coffee to those physicians she had worked with, they were unresponsive. She was now a housewife and mom, not a doctor: it was the common work that had held them together. Retirees who are "people persons," or extroverts, will likely feel the loss of community acutely. On the other hand, they are usually able to make new friends more easily. For those of us not wired that way, searching out new relationships becomes a burdensome undertaking, made more difficult by aging. It's not as though most older people can go out to a bar at 9:00 p.m. and find new folks to socialize with. So we need to find ways of being that work for us.

·······

Humans, like virtually all warm-blooded animals, are social creatures: we literally need interaction with others as much as we need food. From the warmth and protection of our mother's womb, against our will, we are thrust into this world. A tiny newborn, we cry, we protest. Who will protect us? Who will show us the way? The search for love is the driving force of human life—not romantic love alone, although some make a fetish of that, but trusted friends, attachments of all kinds. The source of our emotional well-being is reciprocal relationships. Above all else, that's what keeps the wolf away from the door.

In their profound book, *A General Theory of Love*, three psychiatrists—Thomas Lewis, Fari Amini, and Richard Lannon—posit that although many people assume the body is self-regulating, that is not the case. We talk about a "vibe" coming from another, or an exchange of "energy." The authors call this *limbic regulation*.

We are all, in other words, radically interdependent. Relatedness is not just pleasant or comforting—it is physiologically necessary. We know that if children are fed and clothed, but not held and played with, they develop severe behavioral and emotional problems and may even die. Adults are not as vulnerable, but research shows that mortality is more directly related to relationship than to any other healthy living habit, including diet and exercise.

A study known as the Beta Blocker Heart Attack Trial followed 2,300 men who had survived a heart attack. Researchers found that those with strong social connections had only one-quarter the risk of death of those not socially connected, even when other factors like diet, smoking, exercise, and weight were considered. Cardiovascular function, hormone regulation, and immune systems are disrupted in adults who become separated from others for long periods. Subsequent to losing a spouse, the remaining partner often suffers illness and occasionally even death.

In a fascinating longitudinal study, "Triumphs of Experience," George E. Vaillant followed 268 male Harvard graduates from their teens to old age. Among them were John F. Kennedy and Ben Bradlee. These young men were the crème de la crème: intelligent, sophisticated, advantaged in every way. They had been selected from the rest of the entering class because they were considered the most well-adjusted. Judging from their privileged beginnings, one might expect these men to grow into highly successful, happy individuals. Not so. One-third of the men ended up suffering at least one bout of mental illness. Many would be plagued with alcoholism. Those socially isolated died younger. Those who suffered from depression were much more likely to be dead by their early sixties. Vaillant's final conclusion is profound and instructive: "What's critical," he says, "is allowing yourself to love."

Reading this study, I flashed back to my adolescence. When I was sixteen, I went to the family doctor with a problem. I was sitting on the exam table, swinging my legs, feeling very much unsettled. Dr. Pat asked, "And what brings you here today, Marilyn?"

I said, "I can't love."

He must have been startled and confused. He asked, "Did you do anything bad with a boy?"

"No," I said, shocked and ashamed that he would even ask such a question. "I've never even had a boyfriend. It's just that I can't love anyone."

Dr. Pat said, "Well, Marilyn, I could send you to Shreveport to one of those fellas who deals with this kind of problem, but those doctors are expensive." (I expect he knew there was next to no chance that my father would be driving me to Shreveport, fifty miles away, and paying to see a psychiatrist.) "You're all right, you're a fine young woman. I know there are troubles in your household—when you get older and leave home, you'll feel better."

He was right. I no longer doubt that I can love, but I'm always caught unaware when people express love for me. Admiration, yes—love, no. I've been plagued by depression and feelings of unworthiness most of my adult life. We can leave home, but we never entirely escape home.

I'm remembering the tenth-anniversary celebration honoring me at the church. Various congregants spoke, not lauding my good deeds, but speaking words of affection. The fine choir sang "You Are Worthy." Thrown into full-blown cognitive and emotional dissonance, I buried my face, in tears, in the shoulder of Julia, the rock of a woman sitting next to me.

By the time I retired, I had largely grown beyond this sense of unworthiness, but I remain an introvert. People have sometimes referred to me as "self-contained." Others have used less positive words, such as "self-centered" or "aloof." I don't chat, the usual lubricant that opens social relationship. I dwell most comfortably in the abstract world of ideas—because I'm curious, I like to dive deep. Though age has softened me and has made me more aware of the emotional needs of others, less likely to debate, and more likely to smile and listen, most of my friends are people interested in big-picture stuff, whether it's politics, philosophy, or literature.

......

A consultant who helped our church through a difficult patch told me that my biggest weakness was my introversion. It's true that I rarely attended church social events. I off-loaded staff relationships to my associate minister—fortunately, he and other staff carried most of the weight of social interaction with congregants, and my strong leadership skills and intimate preaching style seemed to suffice to keep the church strong.

The challenge for all of us is to find that sweet spot in a chosen career that is right for us, that allows us to make the most of who we are, with our particular personalities and predilections. I was fortunate to minister in a large church, where I had a sizable staff to handle a variety of tasks. Had I been in a small or mid-size church, where the minister typically wears all the hats, I probably would not have survived ministry.

# 26

## *Letting Go*

New retirees are often taken unaware by the suffering they experience. Looking forward to the freedom, the leisure, the new choices, they are surprised to be confronted with changes that can be soul-shattering. Tal Ben-Shahar, the Harvard-trained positive psychology expert, coined the term "the arrival fallacy"—our overestimating how achieving a positive goal will affect our happiness and well-being. So thinking that a life post-work will be relaxing and joyful—even when retiring at the pinnacle of a successful career—may prove horribly disappointing. Dr. Ben-Shahar says we are "future-oriented" species, so we need to have goals—when life lacks meaning and purpose, an individual is vulnerable to depression and ill health.

In a similar fashion, psychologist Robert Delamontagne, author of *The Retiring Mind: How to Make the Psychological Transition to Retirement*, says that the cultural norm is that retirees are at last living the good life—but many experience anxiety, depression and debilitating feelings of loss and never let others know because they're embarrassed. *How can I be so screwed up? Why am I not happy?*

Delamontagne himself retired at sixty-three from a highly competitive job as an executive in a software company. In researching his book, he talked to other retirees and found that those who were more competitive and assertive, like himself, had more difficulty adjusting to retirement. He believes that the very qualities that make people successful in their work lives often work against them in retirement. Again, I recognized myself.

When I was leading First Unitarian, each morning captured my attention. The days brought frustrations and were not free of failure, of course—parish ministry is not an easy job—but I saw even the tedious tasks and the painful learning experiences as part of the larger whole. I knew I was doing what I was meant to do. My relationship with my congregants was symbiotic: I held them, and they held me, in an embrace of common values, common purpose. I called them "my people." They knew I loved them, and they reciprocated. When I retired, I was uprooted, torn from the ground that had sustained me so well for so long. My research was suggesting that I had a demanding journey before me, a time of exploration that wouldn't be quick or easy: I was thrown into radical questions of meaning and self-worth.

......

After a few months of realizing I didn't have to preach on Sunday morning, didn't even have to get out of bed, I thought maybe I should just volunteer with some non-profit that I admired. I had skills, knowledge. Maybe I could find some place that might benefit from my age and experience. My thoughts naturally went to organizations that provided help to individuals who were suffering or perhaps in crisis of one kind or another. I considered Write Around Portland, where volunteers help disadvantaged people—prisoners, battered women, homeless persons—write their stories. Or maybe I could be a hospice volunteer or a counselor for children who've lost a parent. *Just choose*, I told myself—stop sinking down into misery and indecision and start engaging with others and their needs. After all, that was my modus operandi as a parish minister. But I didn't want to choose, I couldn't. Finally, I realized: *Marilyn, you're still grieving.*

New life can be found after retirement, but for those of us who loved our work, *the transition cannot be made without an emotional/psychological leave-taking.* I had become the perennial high achiever, from my school days forward—but when the framed certificates were given, the degrees achieved, the awards received, I was still the little girl who needed attention, who believed at some deep place in her psyche that she was unworthy. She had made sense of her life by offering her gifts—a ransom, of sorts. *See what I can do? Maybe you can't love me, but you can at least admire me, can't you?* Her modus operandi was ailing, maybe sick even unto death. Not to say that any of this was logical, but then who is driven by logic? Not one of us. At least in those primitive places that matter. I was in a state of mourning. I needed to explore the sources of my sadness and disquietude.

Retirement required me to let go of who I thought myself to be. I felt myself taking a very large leap into nothingness—it was like letting go of the trapeze bar and hanging there in midair, wondering if the next bar will ever arrive. I had been the highly successful minister of a large church—a pioneer of sorts, the first female senior minister since the church was founded in 1866, and one of the first ever female ministers of any large church, of any denomination. I was clinging to my identity, to my virtue, to my pride and self-importance. That was a pile to let go of.

# 27

# *Creating a New Narrative*

Through the years, we develop a narrative about who we are—a story that brings clarity and purpose to our speech and actions, a framework through which we understand the past and anticipate the future. Our story often becomes fragmented when we retire, and familiar patterns of all kinds are broken: daily tasks, companions, finances, goals. That was certainly true for me. To move to a new place of comfort and reliability, I needed to reconsider my personal narrative.

Eight years ago, I joined four others also in the process of retiring—an invaluable experience: my feelings were witnessed and confirmed by companions going through the same changes. The group was started by a woman who had recently retired from an executive position at Intel. Other members included a woman who had been a lawyer for a non-profit, a man who had counseled divorcing couples about finance, a man who continues to work part-time as an investment advisor, and a man who was a client services manager for a socially responsible investment firm.

We share our various stories, laughing and commiserating, as we struggle together to find new ways of being and doing. We confirm that our feelings are not unusual and that we are not alone in our pain and confusion. We learn that we have to acknowledge our losses and to grieve, as a prelude to moving into new arenas of interest and building new structures of meaning. And now we are not without companions as we navigate this surprisingly difficult journey to a new way of being.

All the members of our group are people who held significant positions of leadership in their work lives. Finding satisfaction post-retirement is especially daunting for individuals who have been leaders—they are commonly imaginative and visionary, and these characteristics don't go away after they leave their jobs. If they choose to do volunteer work, they require a setting, institutional or otherwise, in which they can feel free to use their formidable skills. They do not want to collate mailings—they are accustomed to initiating: making policy and moving an organization toward a goal.

Retirement is a kind of leveling force. When you're not in the catbird seat, moving the agenda forward, you are brought down to earth to meet . . . well, none other than yourself, without the wings that allowed you to swoop down and fix things. No longer do you have a ready excuse for your anger, your impatience, or maybe even your bullying behavior, all in the name of "meeting the mission," "getting to goal." You become just a friend, just a neighbor, just a member of whatever group you're in.

Personally, I've had to learn new and more egalitarian ways of interacting, to find ways to contribute without necessarily being a leader or even having a formal role. I'm used to speaking with authority, so I've had to watch the way I present myself—at times I've alienated others with my presumptuous manner. As the leader of an institution, and a minister, with all the sovereignty that accompanies that role, I assumed that I would always be granted audience and that most people would defer to me. Not as readily now, I've discovered.

Our group meets monthly for a long lunch at a restaurant that's quiet enough for us to talk. When the group first formed, one of the most common complaints went like this: "I wake up in the morning, and I have nowhere to go. No one is expecting me. I don't know what to do with my time." As workers, we had played the piper's tune all our lives—we began to realize that now we are being asked to play our own tune. Driven by goals and deadlines, some people have literally never asked the simple question, "What do *I* want to do?"

We begin our informal group by talking about whatever interests us at the moment, whether it's politics, an article someone read, or a moving film. We talk about what's happening in our lives. Recently, one of our members experienced the sudden death of a grown son, so we check in with her week after week to see how she's coping. Another had knee surgery—we witnessed his disintegrating movement for a couple of years, as well as the aftermath of a successful surgery. Still a third has been planning to do a Camino de Santiago pilgrimage—we heard about the preparation and then recently about the completed journey.

Maybe halfway through our time together, someone says, "And how is everyone's retirement coming along?" Then we become more focused as each person gives a kind of check-in as to what we're doing with our time and energy. We've discovered that retirement is a process, and our needs and wants shift and change as we continue to traverse the territory. We end our meeting the way we begin: with warm hugs all around. Then came the pandemic—the hugs stopped, and our meetings were on Zoom. Through these years, we've each had successes as well as bumps along the way. At this point, with the possible exception of Cindy, our newest member, everyone has morphed into a place that seems genuinely satisfying, whether it be volunteering or taking more time to be with a grandchild.

I've asked each member of our group to speak to various aspects of their retirement: difficulties in adjusting, meaning and identity, aging and mortality. Here's what they had to say, in part.

## Randy, retired director of business operations for a non-profit involved in workforce development:

I have a lot more time now to do what I enjoy—to travel and spend time with my family. I have a new grandchild, and he has been a real joy. I also volunteer at the church—I'm chairing the board now. The piece about meaning, though, was a problem at first. I had no trouble filling my time, but wondered about my goals. When I asked myself, "What am I supposed to be doing?" I was depressed and sought out a therapist. I'm taking a memoir writing class, trying to find more peace within myself, more of a sense of well-being. My sense of my own mortality has become more prominent—I've begun to lose friends, but I thought I would never die. I've begun to understand I will—I have concerns about *how* I'll die. My mom had a hard time. I'm learning to look at life by living at the moment. I'm in some ways more secure in who I am, and I have a great opportunity to interact with others now, and be supportive.

## Margaret, retired manager in HR/development at Intel:

I'm proud to retire from Intel—it was a daunting place for women, and I was successful there. I'm an extrovert, and with more time on my hands, I get tired of being by myself and doing something I really don't want to do. Because I'm single, I've depended on my female friends. I enjoy going to the theater, movies, lunches. I'm in a choir, and for me that's the highest form of self-expression, when my pulse synchronizes with others. My daughter is in a high-pressure job, and I've taken over some of the care of my grandson, who is finishing high school. I find meaning in *doing*—I've become a national leader of SCORE, a large volunteer network of retired businesspeople who mentor individuals who want to start businesses. I find that very satisfying—I can apply the knowledge and skills I learned at Intel. Death loomed large for me when I lost my son, who died in his sleep, we're not even sure why. I think I'm more able to die now—maybe I'll see him again, maybe not. I do love to travel, and I'm planning a trip to China, with some friends.

## Paul, recently retired client services manager for a socially responsible money management firm:

Paul, the newest member of our group, retired at fifty-eight about a year ago and moved with his partner to California. Paul is an anomaly in our group in that he seems gloriously happy in retirement. His connection with our group is more based on friendship than a need to deal with retirement issues. Paul is an extreme introvert and is fine being alone. He could be a monk and live in silence.

Fortunately, my transition has been a great one. I was ready to retire, and I've always had more than enough passions and interests to keep myself busy and engaged. The job I did for pay never figured prominently in my identity or my sense of self, so I didn't find myself with a large gap in my life that required major adjustments as to how I viewed myself or my place in the world. My work was always quite fulfilling, but it was also extremely stressful and demanding of my focus. In many ways it was a liberation to be able to step away from that work at a time when I still felt that I was competent and capable. And with a life already packed full of non-remunerative interests (music, gardening, cooking, distance swimming, reading, creating stained glass), I was quite thankful to have such a large chunk of my work week freed up to focus on these activities that bring me so much joy. Financial independence/comfort has played a huge role in allowing me to retire and enjoy other aspects of my life. I feel incredibly fortunate. It is not so with millions of other retirees.

## Pat, retired director of a non-profit involved in workforce development:

After a few months of retirement, I found myself bored and started a business to provide investment advice. This work takes about ten hours a week. I definitely had some issues with identity—for over a year after I left work, I wasn't sure who I was and how I would be perceived. I had a problem with my wife early in my retirement—she works at home as an artist and was used to having quiet, solitary time, and I'm an extrovert, so I kind of drove her up the wall. Volunteer work continues to be important, and I've gotten active with several groups (a men's group, hiking group, meditation group, and our retirement group). Initially, I had a hard time knowing what day of the week it was, but now the issue is that I'm heavily involved in a range of activities that tie me up most days. Overall, I'm happy with my current life. I've redefined what 'productive' means to me: (1) what I'm doing to find joy and (2) what I'm doing to help others. The other area worth mentioning is my spiritual life—I'm in a meditation group, and I've established a set of spiritual practices. My best advice to someone retiring is to think about what's important to you and what gives your life meaning before you retire. Be patient in finding your path—this is a major transition, and you need time to let the path come to you.

## Cindy, retired lawyer, teacher, author:

I was mostly a self-employed, progressive-minded lawyer who worked with LGBT and women's groups. I'm also a historian with a PhD in US intellectual/cultural history. I now do occasional non-profit workshops and presentations related to history. The most significant issues for me are my concerns about health and mortality. I thought of retirement as the step before death, and that was unnerving. I've used my retirement to make a major review of my life and to understand the "story" that I have lived. I plowed through the mementos of my life and now have a much better understanding about what my life's calling has been, and how to hold onto it and live it out. My parents died in the eight years before my retirement, and I was extensively involved with their declines. I will die, but like them, I will also live on in the ways I've impacted the world and the people in it. I'm eager to spend more time with my wife, seeing plays and doing fun things. I plan a trip to Albuquerque on the fiftieth anniversary of my kidnapping during a restaurant robbery. I did not expect to live through the night, but I connected with my kidnapper, who ultimately opted not to kill me. I plan to return to the site of the abduction and see if the man is still alive. I want to thank him for his decision not to kill me. Oddly, it changed my life for the better—on five occasions since, I've been in situations where I was able to interrupt male violence. My nose is sniffing the wind for what's next, and I'm generally feeling very excited about what's to come in my seventies.

······

Talking with other retired people, I saw again and again similar issues being raised: grieving the loss of personal power; difficulty structuring time; searching to find something meaningful; difficulty at home because one spouse was working and the other not; concerns about aging and health. And I saw individuals working through this daunting transition and arriving at a better place: reviewing their life and searching for a new story about identity and purpose; finding satisfaction in relationships rather than in being productive; mentoring others; offering their skills and experience through volunteering;

giving counsel and comfort to friends, neighbors, family members who are struggling; exploring new activities they've not had time for until retirement.

Here's the final statement of a particularly articulate individual I interviewed, a pediatrician who gained a lot of personal satisfaction by helping the families she served. For several years, I've watched her try one thing after the next after she retired (removing tattoos of indigent people, vaccinating people as soon as the Covid-19 shots were available, advocating for an endangered natural area) as she worked toward the satisfaction and peace of mind she was searching for. Then, two and a half years ago, she had a tragic boating accident in which she lost both legs. I've seen her struggle valiantly, heard her despair, been amazed at her resilience.

## Catherine, retired pediatrician:

Losing my legs was a very stark loss of my coping strategy. What had brought me happiness was a supple, pain-free body that loved to dance, to hike, to run. It has required, and continues to require, intense grieving, reckoning, processing.

It has required me to ask myself if life in this body is worth living. The answer that pulls me up and back into life is that I still have people who love me well and whom I love. There are still joyful things to do in this body. There is beauty, awe, mystery. There is communion with others who have been navigating these rocky shoals longer than I have.

One of my life learnings has been to reject the idea that my mother lived by—that everything is OK, everything is fine. Taking this tack made her a sunny person, reassured many people who were anxious and depressed, and fostered joy. For me, this strategy also denied and failed to reckon with the things that are not OK that must be named. It circumvented making amends for any harm that one's actions might have caused.

The challenge for me has been to name those things, feel my negative emotions, to honor them and then to move forward. Sometimes that means having a difficult discussion, sometimes it means acknowledging a wound that has accompanied me my whole life that will always be mine. Sometimes it is feeling despair.

What is necessary for me at that point is to thank these emotions for the truth they embody and when I am ready, to let them go and move on into the day. After all, they are only one lens. Allowing them to commandeer what time I have left, the possibility of this day unfolding before me, is also a kind of emotional distortion.

Being able to learn from the dark how to move toward the light creates momentum for living. I can now walk on the beach, and even in the woods on uneven ground with forearm crutches, and I can walk around the house without any mobility aids. Hope is a discipline. It is a choice we make again and again.

# IV

# Reflecting

# 28

# *The More That Haunts Our Days*

Questions of meaning have a way of rising up and smacking us square in the face at every in-between time of life: leaving one stage, yet not firmly established in the next, we feel lost, with no easy answers. *What happened to the script? I was doing so well!* Young adults, out of school and these days mostly unmoored by marriage and career, often struggle mightily. Many return home as they continue trying to find their way. Midlife is traditionally difficult, as we realize we are no longer young, no longer have endless possibilities. Sometimes people grasp at a new love, build a "dream home," or even decide to have another child. There always has to be a "what's next?" for our energies, some aspiration that leads us on, some vision of a future. Questions of meaning become particularly acute as we age.

In the end of the film *Boyhood*, the mother, having struggled mightily for years, finally arrives at a good marriage and a satisfying career. Her son Mason is getting ready to leave for college. The camera focuses on the surprise playing on her face. Having gone through three troubled marriages, she has finally said no to the demands of men and is now in a position of leadership and responsibility. But having focused all these years on her child's needs, she asks herself, in a moment of vast bewilderment, *Is that all there is?*

Retirement is a different kind of existential threat: one with the whiff of finality attached. When the world gives us a message that we are no longer relevant, our sense of self begins to fragment, taking a toll both emotionally and psychologically. When the story we've been following begins to shatter, we doubt that it will end well. The integrity of the self begins to crumble.

......

What is the "more" that haunts our days? This *meaning* thing—got to have it, else why get up in the morning? Why eat the same old boring breakfast of whole wheat cereal and fruit and low-fat milk every day? Consider the ubiquitous weight loss plans, the vitamins and supplements, the boring exercise routine, the bran muffins! All the time spent bathing and brushing and flossing. Why take care of a body that has such a predictably bad future—loss and decay, then the end of existence? We can hardly take in the truth of our mortality—despair begins to perch on our shoulder, with its unceasing demand: *wake up, wake up*! *Unacceptable, simply unacceptable!*

John Milton, in his monumental poem *Paradise Lost*, speaks of "divine discontent." This uneasiness, this primal longing, is the heritage of all human beings, for we have in our genetic makeup some vague memory of the Garden, a state of innocence and womblike bliss before the Man and the Woman eat of the Tree of Knowledge of Goodness and Evil.

Consider how the story is told in the Bible: "And the eyes of them both were opened, and they knew that they were naked; and they sewed fig leaves together, and made themselves aprons. And they heard the voice of the Lord God walking in the garden in the cool of the day: and Adam and his wife hid themselves from the presence of the Lord God among the trees of the garden. And the Lord God called unto Adam, and said unto him, Where art thou?" All of us, ever after, believers or not, must still answer that question: to whom or what are we accountable? *Where art thou, Adam?*

The biblical story is the poetical version of a scientific, evolutionary explanation. Richard Klein, a Stanford archaeologist, in his book *The Dawn of Human Culture*, written with Blake Edgar, argues that this shift happened about 40,000 to 50,000 years ago, when behavioral change took a great leap forward. Homo sapiens arrived in Europe then and left the first clear evidence of abstract and symbolic thought. They began creating advanced tools, ritually burying their dead, and evidencing a self-awareness that had not been previously seen. It's what some theologians call "the paradox of the fortunate fall": our eyes were opened, and we became as gods—and yet we also became tragic figures.

This was the moment in our evolutionary history that we came to know the concept of time, when we came to know right from wrong and were called upon to make moral choices—and when we understood we were going to die. Our blissful innocence was gone. We are finite beings aware of the infinite—therein lies the "cast-out" feeling, the sense of never quite being at home in this world. The one who has eaten of the apple is a creator himself, who can contemplate the universe and split the atom, yet at the same time will become food for worms one day. This consciousness is hardly bearable.

Some of us become inveterate searchers—artists or philosophers or priests—either by vocation or avocation. We reach for something beyond what we can quantify or touch, but feels as essential as the air we breathe. Perhaps all human creatures long for this elusive unity, for the wholeness we have known and at some unconscious level, remember. Hear William Wordsworth in "Intimations of Immortality from Recollections of Early Childhood": "Our birth is but a sleep and a forgetting: / The Soul that rises with us, our life's Star, / Hath had elsewhere its setting, / And cometh from afar: / Not in entire forgetfulness, / And not in utter nakedness, / But trailing clouds of glory do we come . . . ."

It's like the feeling you get when you're finishing a picture puzzle and there's a piece you can't find. You long to make the picture whole. You try one piece that initially seems the right color, the right shape, but no, it doesn't fit. You turn it this way and that, you try to force it in, but you can't. You can't complete the picture. And though you may not realize it, this picture is but part of a larger picture, and it in turn is part of a still larger picture, and on ad infinitum. Its source lies somewhere before you were born and after you die.

I'm reading Patricia Hampl's *The Art of the Wasted Day*, written during a long spell of grief following her husband's death. Her sensuous, languorous prose becomes a kind of giving over, a relinquishment that is a refuge from her grief. Hampl speaks of her piano lessons as a child, from a nun who kept giving her new music, in hopes that she would be motivated to master it, though she had never mastered the previous pieces. She imagines there will always be another chance. Not so, she finds.

I'm reminded of my beginning each new school year as a child: the untouched white paper with the virgin blue lines, the fresh box of crayons with their only-crayon smell and multitude of hues, standing at attention, waiting for my careful, studied use, as I colored well within the lines. What was this image of perfection I was after? Could I ever become worthy?

I recognized this quest as the same as when I taught English at Benjamin Franklin, a public high school for gifted students in New Orleans. The end of the year came, and of course, it was always wanting: not enough of the crucial lessons taught and learned—and some of my students not reaching the mark of excellence I had set for them. I had to let them stream out the door to summer, unfinished as they were. And yet each fall semester I began once more, with resolutions, renewed hopes of perfection. *Tabula rasa!* I would look at a sea of shining faces, so eager to learn! This would be the *most amazing* year! And on through the school year, with its satisfactions, its high notes—and with its predictable disappointments and regrets. The fantasy of perfection, though, drew me on each year, eager to start again, sure it would be different this time.

Hampl says that once in a while, that ideal connection between self and the world occurs, a relationship fortunate and fleeting. My call to First Unitarian was in this perfect register. When I left the church, my consummate dance partner was gone, and everywhere I seemed to stumble and fall, blundering, knocking into others, feeling other than myself—all in a desperate attempt to get back into the flow of a call, gifts in hand, waiting for a touch to come alive. My ministry was a thoroughly erotic enterprise, and now I felt dead inside. I needed a new call to different undertakings and, more important, to different ways of being. I was being asked to go deeper than I have gone, to be more than I have been.

# 29

# *Dreams Change*

Each year as we age, certain possibilities become more and more limited. This kind of knowing sneaks up on us, though, and then one day we understand that we will never have a child, never be skilled enough to play in an orchestra, never be the CEO of the company, never take that trip around the world.

"Dream always," my wise friend wrote to me. That's the key, is it not? Dreams change, of course. As a child, I wanted a pony more than anything else in the world. Never mind that we lived in town, and the garage would not be a suitable home for a pony, never mind that we had barely enough money for one pair of new shoes each year. My prayers had to change. Good Catholic girl that I was, I prayed to the Virgin Mary, and she sent me a dog. I found this scroungy mutt in the alley behind the filling station near our home, thin tail between his legs, eyes turned away, shivering. I washed him down, picked off his fleas, and loved him for many years to come.

I grew into a high schooler and became obsessed with basketball. The coach noticed that I was tall, good at rebounding, and I imagined myself on the first team. However, I had a major problem—I had no spatial sense whatsoever, so dribbling and passing became problematic. I sat on the bench.

I entered college and filled out a form that asked me, among other things, to name a career choice. I wrote "foreign correspondent." I had grown up in Homer, a little town in N. Louisiana, about 50 miles from Shreveport, and had been to Shreveport only once, when my father took me to buy a second-hand cornet for the school band. I didn't leave the country until I was almost thirty—so becoming a journalist overseas was a little naïve, to say the least. I did, however, become a writer, something that my fifth-grade teacher, Mrs. Crump, had encouraged. She wrote on my final report card, "I hope to see some of your stories in print one day." I discounted that comment, though in fact, her sentiment proved prescient. Not a foreign correspondent, but a preacher, an editor, a writer of personal essays and memoir, and lately, short fiction. Dreams change.

As a young adult, I wanted marriage and babies—a dream I had in common with virtually all women of that era. I wrote in my journal, "I know my destiny is to find a strong, good man to love and to devote myself to supporting him." Reading this now, it's hard to believe that I actually wrote it, but the evidence is there in ink on paper.

The average age for women to marry was nineteen at that time, and so when I moved into my late twenties, I was fearful that I would never have a home and a family. At one point, I considered moving to Alaska, where males outnumbered females 4:1, but then I thought, *did I really want to marry a fisherman and live in a place that is dark six months of the year?* I decided to marry the doctor I'd been dating.

Cultural expectations about women were rapidly changing, though, and me with them. My dream of waiting at the door of the vine-covered cottage for my man to appear each evening came under assault first by Simone de Beauvoir and then by a whole slew of other feminist writers: Susan Griffin, Dorothy Dinnerstein, Nancy Friday, Germaine Greer, Erica Jong, to name a few. Serving as a support person for a busy surgeon was not reconcilable with the person I was becoming.

To complicate matters, by then I had two babies, sixteen months apart, and discovered that I was unsuited to mother small children. Actually, that would be a vast understatement—having not been mothered, I had no model to rely on. And although I didn't quite recognize it, I was something of an intellectual. I was surprised at the immense love I had for my sons and at the same time wondered why I was so terribly unhappy. Their energy, their exuberance played havoc with my growing depression. *What was wrong with me? What had always been wrong with me?*

*I'm on the deck of our condo here in Portland, looking down three floors to the broad sidewalk below, lined with trees and flowering plants, blowing gently in a summer breeze. I see a young mother in a sleeveless blouse and sunglasses. She has parked a pram nearby, and she's holding onto the leash of what looks like a poodle wanna-be and watching her son, who must be around eighteen months old. He goes up to a small tree and feels the bark, touching the roughness everywhere his tiny hands can reach. As he totters away from the tree, he almost stumbles on the rock bed surrounding the trunk, but he doesn't. He goes to the middle of the walkway, holds his arms straight out, and twirls in circles. He loses his balance and falls to the pavement. His mother continues to watch, to see if he's hurt. He isn't, but he is scared and runs to her. She holds out her arms, pulls him into her lap, holds him close. "This is what mothers do, have done over centuries of time," I thought. But the scene reminds me of the endless days mothering my two young sons. I was not like this mother, I was not patient, not serene.*

I didn't want a divorce, I wanted an intact family, for my sake and even more for the sake of my children. But I couldn't do it, couldn't stay and survive emotionally, so I left behind that early dream of home and safety and abiding love. I had to accept that my decision would hurt people I loved, first and foremost my children, but also the kind and decent man I had married, promising to love "until death do us part." Dreams change—mine shattered, left in shards and fragments.

James Hillman, in his book *The Force of Character and the Lasting Life*, speaks of the kinds of fantasies that appear attractive at each stage of life—*anything is possible at first*. We keep articles, addresses, consider future possibilities for work and travel—then at some point, all the fantasies are left behind for our true commitments: we find our place, we find home.

I found my true calling as a minister, and upon retiring from the parish, I married the only man I ever wanted to marry. George is my equal, my partner and my dearest friend.

I say to my spiritual director, *Now that I have George, I'm afraid I'll think I don't need God*. Hardly. Change was rifling through my spirit again, ever more unwelcome. I was tired of paying the price of transformation. But reality bites. I had to pay attention.

# 30

# *What Must I Do to Be Saved?*

When I left the church—the place of so very much deep gladness for me—I had little idea how to once again feel at home, spiritually speaking. The sea closed behind me, and I was left staring at the water, stunned and inert, leaving my Moses complex behind, feeling more like Jonah after being vomited up by the whale. Was this my inflated ego being left behind? Could I adjust to not being "special," as ministers are seen by their flock? What happened to the leadership of the Spirit, on which I had staked my life?

*What must I do to be saved?* The old question, but with a different twist: *what will bring the new birth?* I wondered if there would be more awakenings like my road-to-Damascus call to ministry, times when a crack opens to show the hidden edge of another universe. Or will my days trickle down to soup and crackers, *all soup and crackers.*

Thrashing around blindly, I tried to find my way through the morass in which I was caught. I began to realize that spiritual renewal would require me to give up certain assumptions about myself and others, assumptions that rested in childhood narratives that were still controlling my self-concept, my behavior. If I wasn't "good"—that is, morally pure and saving the world in various ways—then who was I? Had my very success as a parish minister turned into an aggrandizement of myself? Paradoxically, had it led to a kind of hubris that separated me from others and from the sacred, which I knew in my heart of hearts was the only ground to be trusted?

I had led an institution, counseled others, become a strong public voice. Now I was hanging there in space, the next move in my high-flying act nowhere to be seen. Was I at the beginning of a fall that would lead inexorably to decline and death? Or did another stage of growth, new ways of being, await me? Who was this person I saw now in the mirror, the woman with the dark circles growing under her eyes, the woman who had run out of . . . *desire? Faith?* Blind to purpose and direction, I entered the nothingness out of which radical newness can arise. *Eventually.*

. . . . . .

As we face the realities of a changing body and mind, our deep and abiding desire to be rendered whole is dashed at every turn. Parents die, and friends begin to be struck down. *But he was so young!* We are astonished that we have aged, like everyone else: we can no longer go to the doctor, plunk down the $25 co-pay, and say *Fix this, won't you*, then go home confident in our path for healing. Fingers begin to ache with arthritis. Or hearing is fine today, in decline tomorrow. Neural pathways light up along a tendon, and *bing, bing, bing,* your hip has forgotten how not to hurt. Or maybe you've got sicca, a dry eye syndrome that makes your eyes burn and sting—not really curable, just kind of containable, they say, and you'll need to use special eye drops made from your own blood *for the rest of your life*. Damn! These conditions of aging become like friends who hang around for those late-night conversations—they become a part of you, and it seems natural to entertain them.

One day, I was complaining to my psychiatrist about a whole plethora of medical problems—nothing that would kill me, just stuff that cuts way back on the fun in living. I thought that's what he was paid for, to listen to such and lend comfort. He said to me, "After fifty, more and more things happen to your body, and then you die." Reality was setting in. I began to understand what I was up against: I was the protagonist in a universal story, a story that I had in common with all living creatures, a classic narrative that was winding down through loss and more loss and finally to death.

Legend is that Krishnamurti, the Indian philosopher and spiritual teacher was badgered by his students to reveal the secret that kept him so calm and even-tempered. He called them together to give them his answer: "The secret is that I don't mind what happens." Ah, the saving grace of acknowledging *what is*—and accepting it.

I'm thinking of Joan Didion's "On Self Respect," one of the most significant essays of contemporary times. Didion quotes from the diary of an emigrating twelve-year-old named Narcissa Cornwall, who writes that their home began filling with "strange Indians," while the father continued reading and the mother spoke quietly. Fortunately for the family, the Indians were not hostile, the girl reports. They were simply part of *what is*.

*Indians always are*, Didion writes. We have a choice: we can fall into depression and despair, muddling through to the end, distracting ourselves; or we can reframe our experience of aging and create a new narrative, one that leads to our blemished and broken flesh, that acknowledges our experience as universal, and then asks us to "finish well." We are called to bless the world even as we leave it.

# 31

# *Where Does the Light Lead?*

Some people peak in high school—the football hero and the cheerleader, who are at the sparkling center of things until graduation. Others peak in their young adulthood—say, athletes, entrepreneurs, physicists. Still others peak at midlife, when they arrive at a responsible position or when they have developed their craft. As for me, I seemed to be on a constant upward trajectory all my life, with a few blips along the way, in disbelief that I would ever peak.

During my growing-up days in Homer, a small town in N. Louisiana, I didn't think of myself as intellectually deprived—but looking back, I realize that we didn't have books or even a record player in our home, and the only magazines were the *Reader's Digest*, containing summaries of articles which were already shallow before they were abridged, and the *Louisiana Conservationist*, featuring pieces about spawning fish. The *Shreveport Times* was my contact with the outside world. I dreamed of one day going to Shreveport and buying one of the fashionable straight skirts I saw advertised at Rubenstein's. That never happened.

We had excellent teachers, though, and a lovely little town library hung with the heads of African animals some wealthy resident had killed decades ago. I visited this library every Saturday, checking out ten books, all that were allowed. My love of books catapulted me out of Homer: I graduated summa cum laude in college, married well, got several graduate degrees, was chosen Phi Beta Kappa, and finally . . . became the Senior Minister of the First Unitarian Church in Portland, a position for which the whole of my life experience had prepared me. Upward and onward. Always the next big thing.

Strange as it may seem, I had never really considered myself as *aging* or actually being diminished in any way. As the senior minister of First Unitarian, I was always in the middle of the action in the community: giving speeches, being interviewed, helping guide various non-profits, even, in fact, "starring" in a prize-winning documentary film, *Raw Faith*. I had my ups and downs with anxiety and depression, but I handled them with my packed schedule: church administration and preaching, civic activity, public speaking. As long as I stayed busy, I could keep my demons at bay.

At some point, though, I could no longer deny the aging process: my body was betraying me, changing in ways I somehow thought it never would. *After my shower, I stand in front of the bathroom mirror. I raise my arms like Jesus on the cross and the soft flesh hangs there like puffy rolls of rising bread.* My joints had started resenting the cold, rainy weather in Portland. Then there was the time I went to the emergency room with stomach pain the night before a sermon. No, not an ulcer, just stress, the doctor said. Another Sunday, I completely lost my voice. My associate minister had to read my sermon to the congregation. *Lost my voice?* The irony was thick.

We stand the child against the wall, we measure. How much growth this past year? We have a yardstick to go by. As we age, we are increasingly less able to judge ourselves by the common measures of society: beauty, money, power, position. Now we are called upon to shift not only our expectations but our very definition of *wholeness*. The core is character: qualities like honor, dignity, wisdom, prudence, grace, mercy, courage. It's the depth and tenacity of our love. Not always easy to measure. Annie Dillard says that growing older is giving her two precious gifts: softness and illumination. *Ah, yes—to see and to not see, to watch where the light leads.*

The constraints of aging can bring a new focus, help us clarify and deepen values, reframe losses as differences. Maybe comprehending the intricacies of a computer is not the *sine qua non* of existence. Aging allows us to give in ways we could not give in our younger years. The ability to listen well is much rarer and surely much more important.

The question was upon me: *How can I make the most of this next stage of my life?*

# 32

# *When Less Becomes More*

In a lovely understated film, *The Horse Whisperer*, Robert Redford plays the part of a horse trainer with an uncanny ability to heal traumatized horses. He's in his prime, but aware of the passing of years. A woman who has come to him for help watches him work, in awe, and asks if there's anything he's afraid of. He says, "I'm afraid of getting old and not being able to do what I do." *Yes, exactly.*

One common fear of older people—especially of intellectuals and writers—is that our thinking skills will diminish, keeping us from contributing anything of substance in our respective fields. Certain functions of the brain do, in fact, decline—the right brain, the hemisphere that carries novelty, diminishes with age. But the left brain, which holds patterns, is increasingly relied upon, so pattern recognition creates a mental economy which counteracts loss in other brain functions. These generic memories grow steadily throughout life, as does intuitive ability, which is actually compressed and focused analytic experience. Both language and higher-order perception (reflection about meaning) tend to be retained, especially in people with high reasoning ability who have long dealt with complex matters.

I read a lot of magazines and newspapers, so I forgive myself when I pick up a magazine I perused a week or two ago and don't remember the title of an article, or in fact much of the content, and begin to read it again. "Oh, yeah, I already read that," I say to myself. If it's particularly intriguing, I might review it. If not, I turn the page. I'm still good at meta-analysis and judgment—the aging brain gets ever better at this aspect of cognition because experience feeds current thinking.

Twenty-five years ago, I went to the Johnson O'Conner Research Foundation in Seattle for a series of aptitude tests. I wanted to see how best to use myself in ministry and what to ask of my associate minister, who also took the tests. It appears that, compared to most people, I have very few aptitudes—I'm not musical, my dexterity is mediocre, and my nonexistent spatial abilities explain why I still get lost in downtown Portland. But the aptitudes I have were exactly right for my career choice: my strongest aptitude is creativity, and I'm also strong in both inductive and deductive reasoning. My counselor warned me to stay away from meetings because, as he said, process is deadly frustrating to me. *How did he know?* The tests reflected my experience. And these strengths are mostly still around.

What I've noticed about my own writing and teaching in the twenty-five years since then is that numbers can throw me off now, and dense logical arguments are harder to follow. However, my *knowing*—what is generally called wisdom—is growing. As is my compassion. I dwell more in the land of unity than in the land of differences, and spiritually speaking, I am grateful to be there.

My short-term memory is doing what aging does to almost everyone: nouns go first, followed by a steady march of adjectives and adverbs. This is an annoyance shared by virtually all those over sixty. When I'm writing, my brain, especially when I'm tired, doesn't easily distinguish among like-sounding words—for example, meaning to write *more*, I might write instead, *moral*. When I try to retrieve information, I often feel like I'm going through a file, lickety-split, as I once did with library card catalogs, discarding, discarding, discarding, passing by information that "sounds like," moving past "reminds me of," until I finally manage to come upon the name or fact I need. When I'm writing creatively and trying to find an exact turn of phrase that is called for, or the precise word, there's always the online thesaurus, which I burn up with use.

If the truth be known, I've always been a bit "spacy," and I've never been good with names, for some reason—I guess my head mostly floats in big picture clouds. Sad to say, after performing a wedding, the couple would leave my consciousness forever, unless we had some other unique bond. Throughout my ministry, I would oftentimes forget the name of a board member, never mind the names of congregants. Members of the congregation were unfailingly gracious. "I know it's such a big church," they'd say. Aging seems to be making me more of what I already was.

The fact is, I need less information, not more: *is there any earthly reason I need to know about Taylor Swift's boyfriend problems?* Our information-dense culture is inundated with mostly mindless stuff that carries us away from the core to the periphery. My current need is to assimilate and make sense of my experiences, to tie the present to the past, both culturally and personally, to ferret out the themes that have driven my life.

As we age, it turns out, we become better and better equipped to do just that. Before her retirement, columnist Jane Brody shared in the *New York Times* the various ways she is slipping. She says these gradual changes in cognitive function began "decades earlier," but are masked by the brain's massive number of neurons and also by the brain's ability to form new connections throughout life. She says that "forgetting may be as important as remembering," because the brain simply can't contain everything it's exposed to.

Brody refers to the brain's plasticity, its penchant for adaptivity. The comforting news, she says, is that older brains comprehend the big picture, see the relative worth of a concept, and understand why one choice might be better than another. Our lives have more than enough content to draw upon—whereas we may not be able to easily recall names, facts, or figures, we have the wisdom of experience. Slowing down isn't pathological for the brain, any more than it is pathological for a marathon runner to slow down. It's what happens. It's OK.

Our youth-oriented culture and its visual images in magazines and on TV send a clear and unassailable message that youth is beautiful and good, and that aging—or even the appearance of aging—is to be avoided at all costs. "Costs" is an appropriate term: women, and now increasingly men, have "work" done to their faces or bodies, to the tune of over 11.8 billion dollars in 2022. Even women in their twenties and thirties begin the process of cutting and burning and injecting in order to preserve a youthful appearance. I find myself falling into this youth cult at times, feeling pleased when someone seems shocked when I reveal my age and says, "Oh, you certainly don't look it!" Our obsession with youth, though, is not chiefly about aesthetics—it's about death, a topic that is too often prohibited from honest conversation in our culture.

I was surprised to find that researchers of "happiness" have found that older people register higher in the happiness quotient than the young or middle-aged. Part of the explanation may be that emotions are generated differently by the right and left lobes of the brain—negative emotions are linked to the right and positive emotions to the left, which is the sphere we increasingly use as we age.

Perhaps the relative contentment of the elderly is, in part, because older people have had to look for a larger order, a sustaining force, that can reconcile all the contradictions of living, even unto death itself. The finite gives way to the infinite as the measure of things. I prefer this explanation—it's a trail that beckons, that gets wider and easier as I travel.

# 33

# The Season of Loss

One day I am flipping through the *Oregonian*, and I happen upon an article announcing that Brian Doyle, a writer friend, has an inoperable brain tumor. He will die. I send him an email: "How could the most alive person I know be dying?" He writes to say, "Bless you!" His faith is strong, I *feel* blessed. Before I can get used to the idea that he's going to die, he dies.

My warm water exercise class at March Wellness is generally full of women, only women. But one day a young man, a quiet kindly soul, joins us and keeps showing up. He's way, way too thin, though, and one day he reveals to me that he has cancer. He has dreams for his future, talks about what he would like to do when he gets better—like be a counselor for troubled teens. I share my anxiety stuff with him, and one day he gives me the flap from a cardboard box of a supplement he had found helpful. "Try this," he said. "It works for me." Not long after, I notice that he has stopped coming to class. "So where is Pat?" I ask.

"Oh, he died last week," someone says. Now, seven years later, I still have that flap of cardboard in the cabinet below the sink in my bathroom. I'm keeping him with me, *those dark gentle eyes, those long fingers stroking the water.*

The dead from my church keep reappearing—Janis Eliot, Don Watne, Florence Rawson, Ned Hayes. I'll see one walking down a street in Portland or in a grocery store, and then I catch myself—*whoops, they're dead.* Each has left a hole in the sky.

I'm at the Living Room Theater, ready to see a great film, and I run into Jane, a poet friend, a handsome, elegant woman who lost her husband a couple of years ago. I haven't been in touch—I register some guilt, but I'm glad to see her now. She greets me, "Marilyn!" and takes me in her arms. I ask her if she's still writing poetry and she says, "No poetry." She seems vague and distant. Something is clearly wrong. I notice a Hispanic woman, a caretaker, by her side. Jane asks, "Do we need to pay?" and the woman answers, "We've already paid." She turns to me and says, "I'm helping Jane." I hug Jane ever more tightly, promise to see her again. I don't. I wanted to see her as she was the last time I had dinner at her place, full of words and grace, breaking greens by hand into a blue and yellow ceramic salad bowl from Italy, saying, "I love cilantro!" A few months later, a mutual friend calls and tells me of Jane's death. I think of her every time I reach for cilantro at the grocery.

I go to my fiftieth high school reunion in Homer, Louisiana. Back then, I was the ugly duckling, or so I thought, and now I'm showing off my handsome architect husband, not to mention my engagement ring with its quiet good taste and vintage diamonds. *Ha, take that!* Brenda, my former college roommate, greets me on the broad lawn of her home—it appears she married well. Apparently the self-appointed class statistician, she immediately begins listing all our classmates who won't make it this year. Because they're dead. David, the quiet, sweet boy I had a crush on, died by suicide. So did Robert, the boy who had polio and walked with a brace. And four or five more, Brenda says. Illness took others, just the usual frailties of flesh. And accidents. Gladney, who married another classmate, Peggy, had been killed in a car wreck. He never should have been driving a Volkswagen Bug, people said. No protection at all if you get hit.

As we age, we're thrown into what has been called "the season of loss." Mom and Dad are dead. And the aunts and uncles. College professors, mentors. And on and on and on. Where are the older, wiser ones to smooth the path, to reassure? Too much sadness to bear. Sends me inward, into emotional flooding, where I'm of little use to anyone. With each death, a part of me seems ripped away, violated.

History flows through me. Time seems to collapse in on itself—so my lover of twenty years ago seems like someone I knew just a couple of years ago. I sift through family photos. I remember Uncle Lemos, how he and Aunt Sugar used to drive up from Baton Rouge at Christmas to visit, how he teased my little sister, taking his belt off his round stomach, putting it around her twice, proving to her that she was twice as big as he was, then laughing uproariously. Gone. And their daughters, Dee Dee and Carol, too. My high school teachers: Mrs. Tinsley, my French teacher whom we called "bird legs"; Mrs. Desordi, the home economics teacher who taught us girls about the egg and the sperm; Mr. Kendall, the band director whose mean little kid I babysat—are they living or dead? Do the math. OK, dead. I like to think of them still there, just as they were, waiting for me to enter their classroom to say hello and thanks. But they're dead, gotta be. My fantasy crumbles.

・・・・・・

Ernest Becker says in his classic book *The Denial of Death* that it's impossible for us to accept the fact that we will die. Sounds right. How can it not *be*? *Impossible!* Once I was not, then I was, and now I am. Am I not *something*? Do I not have a soul, or am I nothing more than a random batch of chemicals? How can the *me* that I have so treasured and cared for, not exist? The *me* that worked so relentlessly on perfecting myself? Could I really be the next penguin nudged off the ice floe into the sharks waiting below? *Watching the almost full moon tonight, I think, "How could I possibly leave this earth, this blue-black night with its halo of light?"*

At some point, you realize you've been orphaned, and you never guessed you would be without your parents. A great void then appears. You begin to realize that you have no backup—in fact, with all your frailty and ungovernable fears, you *are* the backup—the matriarch, the patriarch. The early question returns: *Who will take care of me?* This is not essentially a question of food, shelter, or nursing care—it's a question of tribe: who is left, who will be the wise one?

You have become, surprisingly, one of the elders. What are you constrained to do, to be, as you move to the end of your life? What have you learned? What is yours to give?

# 34

# *What Gifts Are Ours to Give?*

Much of this book was written during months of protests in Portland that turned violent, causing divisions between people who literally want to "defund the police" and people who believe we need more police. Wars rage abroad, these conflicts very much alive in the consciousness of Americans. Now Donald Trump, a convicted felon, has just been re-elected president, to the surprise and angst of liberals. The divisions in our society have grown only more rigid, less amenable to change.

What can be done to counter all this confusion and cultural fragmentation? When a critical moment like this arrives, we look for moral discernment and guidance from a trusted elder—a sage, if you will—who speaks from a place of careful reflection and sound judgment. We turn quiet and listen to the likes of John McCain, John Lewis, Ruth Bader Ginsburg, Toni Morrison, all of whom are now gone from us.

The sage as an archetype dates back to the Greeks—all six schools of Hellenistic thought refer to the *wise one* who has achieved perfect tranquility. The sage is like the gods, if the gods appeared to us, the Greeks believed. They knew, as do we, that no human can achieve moral perfection; nevertheless, the term *sage* is commonly applied to those who have risen above the earthly strivings of wealth and praise. *They have taken concern about themselves from the center and placed the ideals of love, honor, humility, and service there instead.* As we become elders, these are the values we aspire to.

What are the marks of the mature life? The sage, having found the desires of the ego wanting, is profoundly countercultural. Having been through their own mishaps, mistakes, and miscalculations, they no longer need to project flaws and failures onto others and are therefore free to own all aspects of self. Forgiveness, both of self and of others, finds a broader and deeper dimension—a way of being, not just a single act.

Age doesn't necessarily bring wisdom, of course—wisdom emerges from a life committed to learning and reflection, and accrues with the assimilation of experience, reduced to its essence. But the mantle of sage can rarely be worn by the young, who simply have not suffered enough of life's quandaries—enough failure, enough betrayal, enough loss—to find a comprehensible pattern beneath the chaos of existence. We can aspire to the role of sage only in our later years.

All transitions—those that carry hope and promise, as well as those that carry the burden of grief—invite us inevitably into a new place from which to view ourselves and the larger world. The changes we don't choose and don't want demand the most from us and may offer the most profound form of redemption: we may become kinder and more compassionate than we have known ourselves to be.

The Buddhists use a term, "Great Compassion," inviting us to hold seeming opposites at the same time. Vietnamese Buddhist Thich Nhat Hanh writes of a twelve-year-old girl that is raped by a sea pirate and then makes the startling observation that we must love both the girl *and* the pirate. How do we forgive the mother of the autistic child who shoves her son off a bridge? We begin to understand that it's an act of grace that we're not the ones doing the shoving. "There But for Fortune," as Philip Ochs' song goes. Mercy rises over judgment.

The sage understands that existence is precisely "*what is*," and it's not amenable to fantasies about what should be. This stance is, in fact, the only place from which lasting change can emerge. This fearless embrace of existence *as it is* is not unlike the great theologian Paul Tillich's "ground of being," whether we call it *God* or use some other metaphor. We enter a trust that goes beyond anything within our control—a trust in life itself.

Sagehood is a relative matter, of course. Not everyone can be a Thich Nhat Hanh or a Thomas Merton or a Pema Chodron, but we elders can claim the wisdom we've accrued and support younger people who are struggling with the same human stuff we've passed through. We don't have to be a monk or even very well-read. We don't have to lay any "truth" on others. In fact, it's best we don't. We can begin simply by being fully and heartfully present to another. With this simple spiritual practice, we can "listen someone into being," as Nell Noddings put it. It's a gift of the servant, rare and precious.

# 35

# *Bestowing a Blessing*

An elderly man was admitted to the small hospital where Mark Agronin was interning. The patient turned out to be one of Mark's heroes—the brilliant psychotherapist Erik Erikson, then at the end of his life. Erikson lay in bed, unable to talk, totally dependent on the nursing staff. Agronin recalled once speculating about how Erikson's life would end, and now he was witnessing the final stages of his life. It was painful to be so close, yet so removed. And yet he realized that a deep bond was there, between generations. Agronin understood the enduring connection between the stages of life, he says, and how elders can give us both vision and a blessing. This inestimable gift of blessing is one, in fact, that only the elderly can bestow.

・・・・・・

Where are the wise ones who guided me, opened doors that seemed so firmly shut? They're gone, all gone. What remains is a distillation of the myriad gifts they have bestowed upon me. Now, memories crowd in, reminding me of those who have blessed and sustained me, carrying my life forward: my father breaking small branches off our black walnut tree to shade his tiny new tomato plants from the Louisiana sun; Miss Holcomb, my senior English teacher, touching my shoulder and saying, "Marilyn, you don't have to carry the troubles of the world on your back"; my grandmother in her big blue easy chair, reading her Bible aloud: "Bless the Lord O my soul, all that is within me, bless his holy name," the selfsame Bible I read from now.

I lost my mother when I was ten, and until recently almost all recollection of my life before that fateful day simply disappeared. But now certain memories come slipping back. I woke up this morning from a dream about the slide at the Coca-Cola Park, where I played as a child. *It's my sixth birthday. My little friends have come to celebrate with me, and the braver ones are climbing one by one up the steps of the tall slide, then zipping down. I want to go down the slide, but I'm afraid. I climb oh so gingerly to the top, but then freeze—I can survey the entire park from here, and it seems a long way down. Mother, her dark hair curled around her face, is waiting at the foot of the slide. She is smiling up at me, her arms reaching out, holding the space for me. "Come on, Honey! I'll catch you." I let go and fly down the slide, coming off the uplift at the end, into the safety of my mother's arms.* I wake up, my face wet with tears.

These memories seem to come out of nowhere, seem arbitrary. Why these and not others? And why are they emerging now? Perhaps some kind of strange integration is occurring, some work of the soul. I am all that has gone before: every kindness, every disappointment, every sweet word from another, every trip I took to a strange site, every desperate gesture from a person on the street, every book I ever read, every face remaining fast in memory. Experiences keep coming back, wafting in like uneasy ghosts, as I find places for them in my psyche. They're inviting a wholeness that was not possible for my younger self.

······

I'm at home on this wintry, overcast day with a cold—wonderful! An excuse to sit by the fire and read. I'm thinking about making some biscuits—comfort food from the past. I remember my grandmother's biscuits, incredibly light and fluffy creations I took for granted during my growing-up days. I've tried on many occasions to make biscuits like hers, but I can't.

The next time my sister from Alabama visits, I engage her help. We don't have a recipe because Granny never used one, so we guess at the ingredients. We both remember the Crisco, how her practiced hands worked the lard gently into the flour mixture, how she patted the tacky mass into a mound, how with a few deft moves, she rolled out a circle in just a bit of flour, how she cut the puffy rounds and snuggled them next to each other in the melted butter lining the iron skillet, then popped the skillet into a hot oven. My sister and I try our best, but our efforts fail: our biscuits are hard and heavy.

*Why am I so obsessed with my grandmother's biscuits, so drawn to the image of her hands in the flour?* When I was young, my job was self-differentiation, but now my focus is connection, assimilation. These biscuits feed my spirit.

Going through family letters, I come upon three from my grandfather. As a child, I saw him as fearsome, like an Old Testament patriarch, but now the complexity of his character emerges. Big Papa composed letters on his ancient black Remington Rand, light and medium-light characters uneven on the line. The apostrophe didn't work, so he used a comma instead. The yellowed envelopes are loose, unglued with age, so I take care, allowing the pages to fall gently into my hands. I read and remember. The following one, written not long before his death, is in shaky but still graceful cursive:

*Mother can scarcely get up when she is down but I can get up readily but I have to hold to something or use my stick or I will fall down. But in our condition we neither one have any pains at all, eat, sleep and rest well and I feel we are wonderfully blessed as Mother will be eighty-seven years old Dec. 16 and I will be eighty-nine if I live until Oct. 19th, which is close by, so you see we are in much better shape than most old people. . . . . I can't see well enough to write very much and that worryes [sic] me to a great extent. And I am also so dizzy until I have to use two sticks when I walk out of the house to any distance. I never dreamed of my eyesight leaving me at my young age. Ha. Ha.*

He and my grandmother both died the following year, within six months of each other, he at eighty-nine, she at eighty-eight. They were married sixty-seven years. In their old age, they took in three homeless grandchildren and a semi-wayward son, a massively unselfish and loving act, which I never really appreciated until I reached my seventies and understood that I could not imagine doing what they did.

· · · · · ·

Aunt Mellie, one of my father's sisters, grew up with protruding teeth and no money to get them repaired until well into her adulthood. She struggled with self-respect as a young woman, and like all her six siblings, she suffered from a critical and sometimes brutal father. Aunt Mellie took me in the first year after I lost my mother. I had no clothes to start school, so we went to the Tot 'n Teen shop, the best children's clothing store in that small Southern town, where she bought me two dresses: one with large green and white checks and a sash that tied in the back, the other pink and gray, with tucks in the front. I remember little else from that traumatic year, but I can still picture those garments as if they were given to me yesterday. Aunt Mellie wouldn't allow bad posture or bad grammar—no, I should stand and speak like I was somebody, because I *was*, she said.

Aunt Mellie taught senior English at the high school, so we used to walk to school together each morning. I was so proud to be walking beside her! She became a role model for me—to some extent, a substitute for the mother who was missing. Like her mother, my grandmother, God was a living presence in her life. I learned from these two women that my life was sanctified, that I was beholden to something beyond myself. Bought with a price. More than anyone else, Aunt Mellie saw beauty and goodness in me, and she raised possibility. Every child needs at least one person to do just that. I continued to visit and correspond with her until she died at 93.

A letter from October 1981 reads:

*You are special to me—more like a daughter than a niece. When you are having a problem, I think about you and pray for you often. What kind of writing do you plan to do?*

*One of my college professors told me I should be trying to write, not to teach. I guess we have something within us that is bursting to come out and keeps pushing. I was never up to disciplining myself enough. . . . I think you are different. You have more push and determination than I have. You also have talent, so go after it if that is what you think the Lord wants you to do. If we are in his will, things come out as they are supposed to, not always as we think they should. . . .*

Although my language differs, Aunt Mellie's focus on being "in God's will" is the faith I owned as a child, and still own. I follow, albeit imperfectly, as I feel led: I ask for guidance and watch what turns up—whatever gives me life and joy, and an opportunity to use myself well in the world. When I sense a direction, I say yes. Mostly. *It may be sewing up a torn garment, potting a plant, writing a letter . . . or it may be writing this book.* Aunt Mellie would approve. She would be proud of me.

# V
# Becoming

V

Reckoning

# 36

# *A Great Cloud of Witnesses*

*Therefore, since we are surrounded by such a great cloud of witnesses, let us throw off everything that hinders and the sin that so easily entangles. And let us run with perseverance the race marked out for us. . . .*

— HEB. 12:1

I'm remembering certain turning points in my life when various elders were there for me. Unbidden but somehow appearing at precisely the right time.

At the age of eighteen, I went off to Louisiana Tech, in Ruston, where I majored in English education. Three years later, I graduated, and just then, a teaching job came open in Homer, my hometown. Being the very religious young woman that I was, with a God who was quite a taskmaster, I thought to myself, "Maybe this is a sign from God. Maybe I'm supposed to take this job and remain at home, taking care of my aging grandparents and my little brother and sister."

I made an appointment with Mr. Haley, the Superintendent of Schools. I knew him, of course, because everybody knows everybody in Homer. I had gone to high school with his two sons, Ben and Bob. Waiting anxiously, I noted the bony structure of Bob's face in his father's as Mr. Haley slowly turned the pages of my resume. He couldn't have been old at the time, but he seemed old to me. I think it was the gravitas showing through. He spoke slowly and directly: "Marilyn, you've done well in school, and you are very well qualified for this teaching position." He paused. "But I'm not going to give it to you."

"Why not?" I asked.

"Because you need to get out of this town," he said.

I felt the weight lift from my shoulders. I said to myself, "Thank you, Jesus!" and scampered out, free to start a new life.

······

I think of my English professor at Louisiana Tech, Dr. Fletcher. Although she taught me some sixty years ago, I still remember her face, her gracious manner. She was an elegant woman with aristocratic features: high cheekbones, a straight nose, and gentle gray eyes, her hair pulled back in a loose bun. Even as she aged, she was a striking beauty—she must have been popular with the young men of her generation. But she had never married—her fiancé, it was rumored, had been killed in World War I. I remember a kind of sadness, a melancholy wash, that ran through her features, like the day when dusk falls, or when a lovely melody comes to an end. Her voice was soft and Southern, and her words came with no pretense—clear and purposeful.

Dr. Fletcher saw something in me that I hadn't seen in myself, and she suggested I might go on to graduate school. I had no money, of course—but she explained that I might apply for something called an assistantship, which would provide tuition and a small stipend to live on, in exchange for teaching. I applied to a few schools—and the only acceptance I received was from the University of Arkansas. That first year of graduate work was the beginning of my understanding of what scholarship is all about. I went on to get three master's degrees and a PhD from various schools. Though Dr. Fletcher was a maiden lady, she helped birth me, gave me some of what a mother might have given. She helped me honor my intellectual life, a longing I didn't even know I had.

······

Another time I was saved by the wisdom and caring of an elder: after long years of study and financial duress, I was planning to be ordained as a minister, but as the occasion approached, I was suddenly struck with the notion that I wasn't good enough to become a minister. I wasn't worried about skills, but rather the moral standards that would be required. Once the title of minister is bestowed, there's no way to rescind it, so I knew that forevermore I not only had to carry out professional duties but also live an exemplary life. Aware of my failings—in particular, my failing to love freely and easily—I thought I shouldn't go through with the ceremony, which was a mere two weeks away, at the church in Lexington, KY, where I had discovered Unitarian Universalism. Preparations had been made, ministers and professors invited, friends and family members gathering from afar, plane tickets and rooms arranged.

I decided to bring my doubts to Rev. Gordon McKeeman, the acting president of Starr King School for the Ministry, where I had studied. He was a man whose wisdom was surpassed only by his humility. Sitting in his office, embarrassed to even tell him of my dilemma, I began to softly weep. He waited, and waited some more. Finally, I choked out my question. How could I allow myself, imperfect as I am, to accept the title, the role, of minister? Gordon took a long, thoughtful moment, then spoke the statement which has carried me through all the years of my ministry, through good times and not-so-good times. He said, "Remember that the efficacy of the sacrament doesn't depend upon the purity of the celebrant." That's all. Nothing more was needed. I understood in that moment that I was in service to something larger than myself, that I was offering, with all my flaws and failures, to be a conduit of the Holy. I didn't have to *be* God, just serve God.

······

Even as I carried on my ministry in Portland, the elders in my congregation modeled courage for me, and steadfastness. When the bombing of Iraq began on March 19, 2003—a war based on our government's lies about Saddam Hussein's "weapons of mass destruction"—over 400 people from First Unitarian joined many, many others in Portland and took to the streets, with our signs, our chants. No, we did not stop the war, the needless deaths, the fracturing of alliances in the Mideast—but we took a stand, as citizens are called to do when their government seeks immoral ends.

I remember returning from that first march, knowing we had done what we could, but nevertheless disheartened, when I saw a tiny figure trudging along, alone, with her cane and her sign. It was Bessie, from our church—she was in her eighties by then, with white hair in that bun favored by older women, and a back bent with the various ailments that cause bodies to shrink and bend. I remember a rush of feeling, quiet tears, connecting me to this woman, honoring her as one who had lived through many wars, and who was still saying no to war, still marching, even though participating must have been hard for her aging body. I knew that when Bessie put down her sign for the last time, I would be picking it up, and when I put down mine, younger activists would be there to pick up mine. And so it goes.

We reflect on what we've been given by so many others—most of whom will never know how much they've helped us, given us the courage to carry on. And now it's our turn. What can we give to sustain those who will follow?

......

I'm recalling a time when I was conducting a writing workshop. While the participants were busy with an exercise, a timid, dark-skinned woman, maybe in her late twenties, came and sat in the chair I always leave open for anyone who wants to speak to me. She paused, blinked several times, finally blurted out in all her sweet earnestness, "I just want to know—how can I be happy?"

Her question so surprised me that I sat up straight and declared, "Why, I'm not *happy*. Happiness is way overrated." I can't remember what else I said, if anything. Maybe I tried to distinguish between *happiness* and *joy*. But I was the minister/teacher/authority figure, so she seemed to accept my awkward reply. Eight years later, I saw her by chance, in church. I'd kept such an affection for her through the years, and I think she, for me. We embraced, both remembering that day in the workshop. My dear, lovely child! How I wish I could have given you the secret! But alas, there is none. We are doomed to be wanting creatures.

To give ourselves over to the pursuit of our individual happiness leads to the loneliest place in the world. Humans are ever social creatures who are interrelated in every aspect of our being. It is in relationship—both personal relationship and the communal effort to recreate the world—that we find not happiness but joy: internal satisfaction, a sense of integrity, and whatever peace is possible in our brief lives on this troubled planet. Happiness is a mirage; joy is possible.

# 37

# *Do the Right Thing*

Chelsea, who cuts my hair every five weeks, is a quintessential blonde who doesn't seem to know that her features are perfect, at least by conventional white-person standards. And she's a bit shy. Our relationship goes way back, back to when she was looking for the right guy, and the prospects looked dim. Now she has been happily married for several years and has a young son, Ellis. She is chatting with me, as we commonly do, as she *snips, snips*. I ask her, "So how is Ellis? Is he likely to have a brother or a sister one day?" Her face darkens, she says, "Oh, no—Ellis is going to be an only child." She's quiet, then confides, "I don't want to bring another child into this world we've made." She's worried about climate change, she says. She asks if I heard about the sea turtles. I had not. "The sea turtles froze," she said. She asks if I heard about the birds dying in Hillsboro—again, I had not. She says, "Twenty or so were found dead, and one was a bald eagle. They don't know what killed them." She says she looked at the pear tree in her backyard recently and thought, "I might need that tree for food."

"What do you mean?" I ask.

"In case our society falls apart," she says.

"You think one day there'll be no rule of law?" I ask.

"What's that?" she says.

I choke, trying to answer.

. . . . . . .

Knowledge is exploding, while wisdom lags far behind. Of all the changes we currently face, that of a warming planet is the most unnerving: *the twenty-first century is the first time in the history of the world that one generation has been given the task of keeping our planet viable, not just for ourselves but for generations to come.*

I see young children walking with their teacher here at the South Waterfront, where I live. There they are, smiling and innocent, dressed in colorful rainwear or sun hats, depending on the weather, a string of them toddling across the street, all holding the rope their teacher has given them so she can keep them safe. How can we fail to understand that *our primary job as grown-ups is to keep our children secure?*

My poet friend Dianne and I are meeting again over coffee, as we used to do once a month before the pandemic kept us trapped at home. I consider Dianne an uncommonly wise woman, and so I venture the question that's pulling at me: "What do you think? Will we act in time to avoid climate catastrophe?"

She smiles wryly, shakes her head, answers with a vast understatement: "Humans are a very flawed species."

There is a great, growing lament in me as I contemplate leaving this world in its present condition, with tribalism rising fast all over the world; with threats to democracy that are real and imminent; with the gap widening between the desperately poor in our country and the flagrantly, insanely wealthy; and most concerning of all, with carbon continuing to rise, threatening a livable future for many species, including our own. I fear that our children, and for sure, our grandchildren, will be living in a world rife with conflict and suffering, as people struggle to escape the consequences of climate change. The younger generations are frightened and angry. *Why didn't we do better?*

Homo sapiens are notoriously unable to consider future consequences. We smoke cigarettes and then wonder how we got that cough. We build next to a vacant lot, never imagining that some new structure will be built there one day—until we hear the roar of the bulldozer. The young rush past their elders in the swim lane, yell at slow drivers, for they can't imagine a time when they themselves will be slow. One day they will find themselves in a rocking chair on their front porch, surprised that they got old. *Hey, it's either die young or get old and then die.* How will they support themselves as they grow increasingly frail? According to the US Census Bureau, 50 percent of women and 47 percent of men between the ages of fifty-five and sixty-six have no retirement savings at all.

Our lack of imagination, in fact, may be what does us in as a species. Scientists have been spelling out, in stark detail, what we are doing to the planet for years and years and years. In the late nineteenth century, scientists first argued that human emissions of greenhouse gases could change the climate. In the 1960s, the evidence for the warming effect of carbon dioxide became increasingly convincing, and by the 1990s a scientific consensus arrived: humans were causing the emissions that resulted in global warming. In 2006, Al Gore's film *An Inconvenient Truth* came out, with startling statistics that few wanted to hear, though to give him credit, he presented his slide show over 1,000 times, all over the world.

Each year, the predictions from the UN Climate Summit grow more dire. June of 2023 marked the hottest sea surface in history. In July, we saw the hottest days ever measured on the planet. And 2024 promises to be even worse. The media typically cover a localized flood or fire but don't generally explain to readers or viewers the connection to that event and climate change. They don't tell us that we're facing a climate crisis and an ecosystem collapse. The newspapers report heavily on movie stars and sports and fashion and food, while not warning the world about the most formidable crisis humanity has ever faced. In the United States, television news is the worst offender: in 2022, ABC, NBC, CBS, and Fox spent just 1.3 percent of their broadcast time covering climate change. They focus on whatever the algorithms say gets the most clicks. My dreams invite fear.

*I'm vacationing at the seaside. I wander around the town, there are no good movies at the metroplex. I feel alone. I start to check out of the hotel, and I see the sea in turmoil. My car is the only one left in the lot by the sea. I understand that I can't make it home in my rowboat. I wonder if my father will come and get me.*

On July 29, 2015, the whole world watched as thirteen Greenpeace activists dangled from ropes tied to the St. John's Bridge in Portland, Oregon, red and yellow streamers catching the wind. They were blocking the exit of the

*Fennica*, Shell's icebreaker headed to the Arctic to facilitate drilling. These young activists hung there for forty hours in makeshift platforms and slings during some of the hottest days on record before the police and Coast Guard brought them down. A hundred feet below them, filling the river with their colorful small boats, were Portland's "kayactivists" from our local Climate Action Coalition—some were experienced paddlers, others kayaking for the very first time. Over 500 people stood on shore, cheering and chanting "Stop that boat!" Some were moved to tears by this unprecedented spectacle and by the courage of the protesters.

I talked with one of the Greenpeace activists who suspended himself from the St. John's bridge. He was in his twenties, I guessed, with platinum blond hair, green eyes, and a smile that won't wait. He lives in New York. He said he got a call asking him to fly immediately to Portland to help block the *Fennica*. He didn't think twice, he said—he got on a plane right away. I asked him why he was willing to travel clear across the country and sit in a sling 100 feet above the river for forty hours in unbearable heat. He just looked at me as if I had asked a very silly question. "We have to do something," he said.

I open the *New York Times* each morning, wondering what new climate disaster will be revealed. Today I read about the calving of a great piece of Arctic ice. The United States should be leading the world in slowing climate change but has been doing just the opposite: giving subsidies to oil companies, the greatest source of pollution on the planet. Both Obama and Biden tried to regulate the fossil fuel industry—but so far the worldwide economic forces arrayed against such efforts have proved too great.

The oil industry started researching the effects of their products on climate as early as the 1950s. As early as 1959, their own research showed the connection of the burning of fossil fuel to climate change, a conclusion confirmed without a doubt soon after that. And how did Exxon and the other oil giants respond? With denial and disinformation. It was almost forty years later that the industry finally acknowledged the scientific consensus and began offering mitigation—which many see as "greenwashing." *Want a good definition of sin? There you have it: selling out the health of the planet and its inhabitants for a little cash.*

The last UN climate conference in 2023 took an important step—195 countries signed an accord agreeing to transition from fossil fuels "in a just, orderly and equitable manner" while "accelerating action in this critical decade, so as to achieve net zero by 2050 in keeping with the science." However, there are no enforceable timelines and therefore no way to ensure if or when significant action will be taken. Elizabeth Kolbert, a leading environmental writer and the author of *The Sixth Extinction*, writes that by the middle of the century, a likely scenario finds the world warmed by two degrees Celsius and almost three degrees by 2090—in which case, temperatures will rise by 3.6 degrees Celsius—or 6.5 degrees Fahrenheit.

Wonder why we have so many apocalyptic films and books just now? Because art is prophetic. In our own lifetime, Arctic ice is melting at an unprecedented rate, coral reefs are dying, wildfires are burning out of control, climate refugees are fleeing for their lives. We don't have years to respond. If I sound agitated, well, I am. I am hopeful by nature, but I am also a realist, and I figure we're in for a pile of trouble.

If we don't address climate change soon and decisively, we'll see more island countries and more coastlines go underwater. We'll see an even greater increase of floods and fires, food and water shortages that will make the current immigrant crisis seem like a cakewalk. We will see increases in tribalism and armed conflict as suffering and frightened people vie for control of increasingly limited resources. Authoritarian governments will rise as democracies lose the power to make people feel safe. The world that our grandchildren will almost certainly inherit is inconceivable to us now. Civilization itself is at stake.

・・・・・・

I am an advantaged white woman living in a high-rise condo on the Willamette River in Portland, Oregon. I use up a whole shitload of resources. I see the rising pile of recycled paper and bottles and cans languishing in the two bins in my pantry, and I think, "I'm eighty-two—this is not good value." Keeping me alive, I mean. How can I sit content? As I write, my fear ratchets up, my breath grows shallow. I can hardly bear the thought of dying and leaving the natural world in the condition it's in. I fall asleep too often with guilt under my pillow.

Greta Thunberg, a young Swedish climate warrior, is not the only child who knows that "the world is on fire." Once I was at City Hall in Portland, along with dozens of high schoolers, testifying about a climate issue. One young woman looked directly into the eyes of the mayor and City Council members and said, "How would you feel if someone told you when you were in high school that the earth would not be a viable place to live when you grow up?"

We can't allow ourselves to look away, to give up. We are already facing disastrous consequences, but perhaps we can still prevent chaos. There are hopeful signs: California, the most progressive of our states and the fifth largest economy in the world, is now producing 100 percent of its energy for long periods of each day with solar and wind. Those of us who have left our careers and enjoy good health have many choices as to how we use our time. Yes, read those books you never had a chance to read. Take up a hobby, like woodworking or photography—whatever might bring you joy. But just now, I'm making a naked plea: please weigh in on the climate crisis.

People typically say, "But what can I do, with such a vast problem?" True, no one can do much alone. But we're not alone: consider the demographic rise of the elderly—we have the numbers to make revolutionary change. Over and over I read, "We know which actions to take to heal our earth, but we lack the political will." As general concern about climate rises in this country, people offer token solutions like buying an electric car or recycling paper and food scraps. So sure, go ahead and recycle, or plant a tree, or cancel that flight to Europe this summer—such individual acts can be a powerful witness. *But much more important than any individual act is political pressure.* Join any one of many organizations pushing in the right direction (see activist/author Bill McKibben's organization Third Act, expressly for older people). There is where you will find companionship, support, direction. And most important, get involved in politics and support candidates at every level—city, state, and national—who are trying, in the plainspoken title of Spike Lee's great film, *to do the right thing*.

We elders will not be around for the direst consequences of our misuse of the earth, but let us do what we can in the years we have left. And then pray for a miracle. *Those of you who still pray. It gets harder, doesn't it?*

# 38

# *Continuing to Minister*

You can divorce yourself from a person, but you cannot divorce yourself from ministry—once ordained, always ordained. That understanding was part of my reluctance to take on the title of reverend. For better or for worse, usually the latter, I am a stand-in for God. I have to watch my language, my clothing, and certainly my behavior. What I do reflects on ministry as a whole. Reflects on God. I get that, I own it.

I continue to minister in retirement, but differently from the formal ministry in the parish. I rarely give interviews, even more rarely do I preach—just three or four times since I retired. I could seek out more preaching, but I don't—I've never liked preaching to strangers. For me, the sermon is a relational event with people I know and love. The last few times I served as a guest minister, I preached a sermon ironically titled "The Meaning of Life." I begin by laughing at my title, but then go ahead and take a shot at it—it's everyman's question, is it not?

I continue to do a few weddings for people I knew, like Chelsea, my hairdresser, and for one of my former congregants, a young man who had been recently released from prison and was starting a new life with the woman who waited eight long years for him.

I did a memorial service for a prominent lawyer who died by jumping off a bridge, shocking everyone except his wife, who knew he suffered terribly from depression. He left a message with his intentions on her cell phone—she and his teenage son frantically called him, but it was too late. His family was without a church home, so a friend of a friend called to see if I could help. The funeral was packed with over 300 people, all confounded, wondering *why*. *He always seemed happy, such a good-natured guy*. People are deeply shaken by this type of death. I started the service by saying that he died by suicide—that's the elephant in the room that has to be acknowledged. My job was to help them understand, to grieve, to walk out a little less unsettled.

No longer am I the visionary calling her people to a new way. I'm finding new ways to contribute, generally not from the front lines, but with the support troops. I do show up with my ministerial stole, indicating clergy, at some demonstrations, or when I give testimony at formal hearings. The cloth still carries weight, and I use it to claim power in the service of justice.

Over the years, I have developed relationships with establishment figures in the community, people with political power, so at times I've been able to open doors for young activists. I didn't even realize I had this advantage until someone in a climate group says something like, "Does anyone know Jeff Merkley?" or "Does anyone know the mayor?" and I might be the only one to raise a hand. I most often simply show up at meetings, listen, nod my head and smile, and try to ask the right questions at the right time to move the agenda forward. Sometimes I can contribute a context, a long view, that is helpful. But these younger change agents will be carrying the day, and I need to follow their lead.

Once in a while, people seek me out for counsel—friends, acquaintances, strangers. I am sometimes called on to consult with younger leaders about institutional problems they encounter. A member of my women's group lost her mother and asked to meet with me. The last time I had an eye exam, the doctor, a garrulous young woman, kept interrupting our session to tell me at length about her leaving a troubled marriage and her life as a single mother. I was glad for her trust in me simply as a caring listener.

Sometimes people ask me to pray for them—such a request always touches me deeply. I was waiting outside a restaurant for George to pick me up, and a man rolled up in a wheelchair, an aging hippy with a red bandana across his forehead, Willie Nelson style. I said, "How are you?" and before long, he was telling me about his life as a veteran. He just needed to talk. When George showed up in our red Volvo, I stood to leave, and the man said, "Pray for me." A member of George's running group, a committed Jew, asked me to pray for him as he anticipated going in for heart surgery—he asked in a playful way, but I knew he meant it. I told him I would keep a candle burning for him for the duration of the time he was in the hospital, which turned out to be eight days rather than the five he expected. I'm humbled by such requests and more than a little disconcerted.

Petitionary prayers feel . . . a little unseemly: *should anyone ask God for special favors?* But I offer them as a desperation move for myself and for others when I don't know what else to do. I don't have any magic, and I'm not even a nice person sometimes, so who am *I* to pray for another? But I still wear the cloth, so I pray as I can. Imperfect as I am. Maybe my prayers are like throwing sand into the wind, but how can I refuse? And in that case, how can God refuse?

I have been active as a volunteer for Ecumenical Ministries of Oregon (EMO), a statewide organization of churches that has as its mission direct service as well as advocacy, particularly in the state legislature. I've given a couple of keynote speeches for EMO on Advocacy Day, when volunteers lobby legislators, but I'm most active on the Development Committee, where I've served for eight years, helping to raise money. EMO serves a huge number of people—immigrants, HIV patients, homeless people, hungry people—on a shoestring budget. In the past, I've done a little fundraising and advisory work for Ceasefire Oregon and Oregonians for Alternatives to the Death Penalty.

······

For many years, I've been an informal student of Buddhism, reading Pema Chodron, Thich Nhat Hanh, Sharon Salzberg, and others. I'm drawn to the Buddhist concept of "skillful means," by which to measure my speech and behavior. I have always had a tendency to speak *ex cathedra* when I give an opinion or weigh in on a decision. It's an occupational hazard of the teacher/preacher, of course, but also finds its source in my childhood insecurity—believing that no one will listen to me now, because nobody did then. Starting with humility would be a good beginning. Listening instead of speaking. Waiting and watching instead of speaking and acting impulsively. When in doubt, considering love as a solution.

I also find useful the Buddhist acceptance of "what is" as a place to begin from, instead of "I shouldn't suffer this way" and "things shouldn't be as they are." I've been dealing with a torn tendon in my hip for several years now, with a plethora of medical treatments that have left me with chronic pain which wakes me in the night. A solution has evaded my doctors and physical therapists. It's difficult to not let this condition dominate my life. My learning, spiritually speaking, is to continue to address the injury without overriding angst and emotional pain, exacerbating the physical pain. There's a certain freedom that comes with acceptance.

One of my greatest pleasures in retirement is my teaching at Maitripa, a Buddhist college in Portland. I marvel at the peace and beauty I experience when I enter this sacred space. I helped them create an interfaith conference, and they recruited me to teach on their adjunct faculty. I'm not Buddhist, of course, so I'm limited in what I can offer, but most of their students are Western, many with a religious background in Christianity, so the dean thought my perspective would be useful. My combination of the PhD in theology, plus the extensive practical learning I bring from my experience in the parish has worked for them. I co-taught a class in compassion with Rinpoche Yangsi, the wise and humble founder of the Maitripa, in which we compared and contrasted Buddhism and Christianity. I've taught homiletics several times because these students want to learn how to articulate their faith more effectively in a Western setting, including the interfaith arena. I'm also a sometime policy adviser to the dean and the director of programming as they create their M.Div. program and work toward accreditation.

I have little interest in lecturing. I find that posing questions is better at provoking learning, and therefore they have become my chief modality as I teach. And of course, I use story. (Well, if it was good enough for Jesus. . . .) I was interviewed on Oregon Public Broadcasting, along with an imam and a rabbi, as to our views on justice, prescribed by our respective religious doctrines. The two men spoke in abstractions, eloquent though they were, but when it was my turn to speak, I always started, "Let me tell you a story . . . ." I told the interviewer, "My main man is Jesus." Yes, Jesus, with his life-giving, straight-shooting stories.

・・・・・・

George and I have lunch every day at the Old Spaghetti Factory here at the South Waterfront, near where we live—we've become part of their community over the years. We keep up with the young servers, who seem to treat us like doting grandparents, sharing their struggles, their dreams. Just today, Jeremiah, a stocky football player at Lewis and Clark College, told us his story. He spoke rapidly, words running together, as if he was perhaps using too much of our time, interpreting for us the tattoos covering his arms. One has the face of his mother, he said, in the veil of the Virgin Mary. His mom moved to Germany when he was thirteen, and he had to take on much of the leadership of the family, because his father and his brothers and sisters were unable to cope. He told us that his mother came home for a visit this past year to see him play football. He said, "I love her so much!" I asked him to stay in touch and give us the fall football schedule, so maybe we can see him play. I told him that I was separated from my mother when I was young, and I know how hard that must have been for him. He was smiling broadly as he left our table. I was moved to tears. *That dear young man!*

······

I've begun to question the very definition of work. Most of the labor of women, throughout time and place, has simply been in the service of sustaining life. Stir the cornbread, make it sizzle in the skillet; mop the floor one more time, where the cat threw up; wash the poop off the baby's bottom, put her in a dry diaper; write the note of condolence to one in grief; take the casserole to an ailing neighbor.

The dad teaches his daughter how to change the oil in her car. The neighbor says he'll water your garden while you're away. The great-grandmother takes the new baby in her aged arms. She is mostly confined to her big easy chair now, for getting up is a challenge. She takes the child, oh so carefully, supporting his neck, holds him on her lap, facing her. She looks into his eyes, celebrating his delicate beauty, his very existence. She begins talking to him, cooing sounds that go beyond words, the infant breaks into a crooked smile. "Ahhhh," say the parents as they look on, beaming.

When do we stop creating, giving? Who among us doesn't work, and isn't all such offering holy stuff? We do it however we can do it.

*I am in my old home in Irvington, a Portland craftsman, where I lived before I married George. I hear a noise on the front porch. I go out and find a policeman trying to help a homeless person, who is being difficult. I talk to him, soothe him, take his face in my hands, kiss him on the cheek. He seems satisfied and goes on his way. The policeman says he used to hear me give advice on TV and he really enjoyed my show, asks me why it ended, I tell him it was the economic downturn. I return inside and see a bouquet of flowers, small but exquisite, in a clear glass vase. Someone wants to give me a large bouquet, but I really don't need it. The small one is just right.*

# 39

# *Ministry of the Word*

I have always seen my writing as a form of ministry—that is, one way of loving. And now, writing has taken center stage.

My position as a parish minister required a lot of writing and speaking, so I was able to indulge my love of words. Besides speeches and articles, I wrote two or three sermons a month, each of those requiring at the very least a day of research and a day of writing. When I retired from the pulpit, though, there were no crowds waiting for my words of comfort and inspiration. It was just me in my study, with pencils and paper, computer, and books. I had the leisure to choose when and what I wrote, but I had no sure audience.

*Where is the awakening she longs for? Where is her true voice? She must be patient, she thinks. Answers will come. She trusts the promise that she will be partnered as she writes—then again, she has her doubts. Maybe with age, the line connecting her with the Guide gets rusty, maybe even breaks. She recalls the brass plaque in her study: Vocatus atque non vocatus deus aderit (Bidden or not, God is present). No, the promise is there. It's the same message that Carl Jung had carved, in Latin, over the front door of his house in Kusnacht. Remember, believe.*

Some writers say they write simply because they love the process. I understand that sentiment, but I also write to give a gift, to complete the circle. On my desk, next to my computer, I keep a reminder suggested to me by Sarah Manguso: "The purpose of a serious writer is to keep people from despair." As a minister, I learned that every human being is beset with a full measure of pain, and many live with despair. My yearning, maybe foolish, is to be a kind of catcher in the rye.

Timothy Egan, in his book *A Pilgrimage to Eternity*, tells the story of Erkembode, the Saint Who Walks. Erkembode traveled through Europe trying to convince nobles to give land to the poor. His legs gave out, and he became crippled. Now children who can't walk make a pilgrimage to Saint-Omer to leave their shoes atop the tomb of the Saint Who Walks. Children do not walk because of it, Egan says, but they learn they are not alone, and they leave with hope. Perhaps the real miracle is the passing on of hope. This is why I write.

Publishing, then, becomes a significant part of the process. It's not a process that typically nurtures, though. Receiving a rejection is tough, and it's even tougher when an editor doesn't respond at all. I know that such disappointments are part of the life of every writer, but my self-doubt gets fed a major meal every time I reach out to get my work published. *The would-be publisher sits on the writer's shoulder, grimaces, and says, "Do you really think this piece of shit could possibly hold anyone to the page?"*

During my ministry, I edited two anthologies of poems and two of essays, for Beacon Press. Plus, I wrote a lot of articles and essays for print and online publications, including the *Huffington Post*. The first book I completed in retirement was a memoir titled *Raw Faith: Following the Thread*. My literary agent thought I might get several offers and would have to choose among them. But that didn't happen. *Beautiful writing, but not a strong enough through line,* editors said. *A rejection, then another, and another and another.* It comes down to the marketing department in the end.

Last year, a publisher did pick up my book of short-short stories, *In Time's Shadow: Stories About Impermanence* (Skinner House, 2019). I spontaneously began writing these short pieces before I recognized that they were part of a relatively new genre called flash fiction. They were fun to write, and I watched my skill develop over a couple of years playing with this form. A second volume, *The Revenge of the Whale* (Fuller Press, 2024), has been published on my own press.

I write all the time, or think about writing. I write letters to the editor, opinion pieces, articles, stories. I journal. Sometimes I wake from a dream and record it before it slips out of my consciousness. I copy perceptive passages from poems, articles, books. Certain lines from films. The shape of a nose might intrigue me. A piece of clothing. The light opening a new day. Dusk, especially dusk, draws me.

Even when the vagaries of life take me away from my writing, I think about what I will write next. Or what I might write about the thing that pulled me away. Every experience is a potential story or article or letter to the editor. I like to edit, to juggle words, to look up definitions from multiple sources. Searching for the right word is a transformative process in itself—words are agents of healing, of transformation.

If the truth be known, I'm genuinely happy only when I'm writing. Writing is my access to the voice of the Holy within, my absolutely necessary spiritual practice. I can't afford *not* to write. As I settle in place, giving myself to the silence, I feel the shift from secular to sacred: my breath slows, my heart rate slows, the disparate elements of my consciousness all start cooperating as one. It's the ground of my being. I'm home.

The haunting of the dark figure with the scepter, the sure knowledge that he's stalking me, drives me to create, for to create is to invite life—to evade the destruction of the body by honing the soul. Rust but also diamonds. When an old woman makes love, she makes age and fleshly decline irrelevant, and in these moments, leaves earthly limits behind. And so it is for the artist—the painter, the singer, the writer, or anyone who creates: we go beyond any constraints of time and place into the infinite, becoming connected with the spheres.

······

*The writer is standing at her laptop in a beach house in Neskowin, on the Oregon coast. Neskowin is a sleepy community of a few permanent residents, but mostly part-time residents and visitors. The only commerce occurs in a couple of restaurants and one finely stocked convenience store. People come here to get away, away from the race to nowhere, away from the endless sales pitch of the culture. She comes here to find out what she's thinking when she's not thinking the thoughts of other people. When she's not trying to fit in, finish her "to-do" list, and oh yes, save the world.*

*She wants to write a book on retirement, a book that someone like herself, lost and longing, would take pleasure in reading, a book that might bring if not direction, then comfort, inspiration. A consecrated book, given with the same purpose as the bread and the wine: new life, forgiveness. She doesn't know if she will be able to deliver, and that thought makes the day grayer even than the winter light, colder than the wind that whistles through the loose window frame as she tries to sleep.*

*The writer has learned that she, like all writers, all artists, will fail to shape a gift as true, as beautiful, as she wishes. Not possible. In her lifetime, the writer has read books that have shaped her thinking, her way of being in the world, books that will never leave her. She despairs of her own gifts. She decides to try to write the book anyway, not someone else's beautiful book, but her own book. It will not be the book she would have written last year or the book she would perhaps write five years from now. It is the book, the only book, she can write just now. She has to sing with the only voice she has.*

# 40

# A Journal of the Plague Years

> *... the infection was propagated insensibly, and by such persons as were not visibly infected, who neither knew whom they infected or who they were infected by.*
>
> DANIEL DEFOE, *A JOURNAL OF THE PLAGUE YEAR*, 1722

The coronavirus pandemic surprised us, starting slowly in January of 2020, engendering disbelief as it quickly picked up speed, then went racing ahead, triumphant. *It will be over soon, surely it will.* But it was not. For me and for many writers I know, our writing remained hopelessly sidelined by the death and dying, the fear, the isolation, not to mention the bizarre political turmoil. *Never mind wearing masks, oh yes, you must wear masks. Wash your groceries down, whoops, no, the virus is airborne.* We watched as Covid-19 spread, not only in our country but throughout the world. We saw doctors and nurses struggling heroically to save people from a virus with largely unknown parameters. We saw refrigerated trucks fill with corpses. For some of us, writing seemed beside the point.

During the entire duration of the plague, I put away this manuscript. Way too much static in the brain—like a bad radio connection in a storm. I read the stats in the paper each morning; watched TV news at 6:00 p.m., incredulous; went out on the deck and sounded my temple bell at 7:00 p.m. every evening, along with the ringing, clanging, chiming of many other condo dwellers, to support the frontline workers—once each day, I made that brief, sweet sound of connection. We became fearful of friends, extended family, grocery stores, even walks in the park. *We stayed in, stayed in, stayed in.* At least those of us who could afford to, those who didn't have to support the infrastructure that kept the rest of us alive. We lived like this for endless months. *Oh, is it Sunday again already?*

Like other couples, George and I had to adjust to being together *all the time*. We're fortunate, though: we had a comfortable, spacious home, healthful food to eat, and most of all, each other. I checked in on my single friends from time to time because I couldn't imagine how I would deal with being alone, without the ability to seek out companionship in the flesh.

My creativity came down to cooking a new dish, or even, for god's sake, straightening the pantry. Maybe writing a note to a friend. I spent a lot of time scouring the *New York Times* every morning, trying to make sense of something that defied sense. I read *The New Yorker*, *The Atlantic*, and *Harper's*. *What do very smart people make of this?*

Every night before sleep, I read for an hour or more—not my usual spiritual stuff, as it began feeling all too distant from real life. Rather, I read lots of history and social analysis, trying to understand why the world felt so unstable, so unsafe. As always, the well-written word was my refuge, offering beauty and meaning to help me make sense of my experience. I wasn't crazy, *everybody* was crazy, so crazy was not my problem. Covid-brain confusion was an existential reality and a completely reasonable response. I could put down my reading and sigh and go to sleep.

The pandemic convinced whole populations of this truth: *all of us need other people—actually quite desperately*. Multiple studies show that a rich social life—not exercise, not eating right, not losing weight—is the single most important factor in staying healthy. At times in our lives, our community disappears: when we move to a new city; when we divorce, and our friends are all couples; when we decide the church we've attended for years is no longer is right for us; and of course when we leave our place of work. During such transitions, we realize how unequivocally interconnected we are and how depleted we become—not only emotionally but physically—when the larger community that holds us is suddenly missing from our lives. I'm thankful we have technology that connects us—like many others, my technical expertise has increased, and Zoom has not been insignificant. But the internet is a poor substitute for human flesh, with its skin tone, its telling posture, the blink, blink of an eye that gives us reams of truth. Technology will let us tell, but not touch.

And then, just as we thought we were coming out of the dystopia we've been living in, we were thrown back into a new wave of infection. George and I love going to the cinema, then to a restaurant to converse about the film for an hour or two. We were just beginning to do that again, just starting to tentatively socialize with a few friends. I even had a birthday party that brought relatives from afar during that brief period of remission in the summer of 2021. Then we were hit with the very contagious variant. Along with most everyone else, George and I pulled back again, even though we'd both been vaccinated. Masks were retrieved, plans for the Portland Lecture Series stalled, trips to the museum canceled.

Each morning during the reign of the pandemic, the first thing I would do after getting out of bed was sharpen my pencils, the ones I used the night before, so I could start over—again and again and again. *Just starting over.* Sometimes that's all we can do, or promise to do. *Hey, I'm still here!* It occurs to me that the isolation we experienced was like retirement on steroids. *How can I give? How can I share the life that is mine, touch into the common humanity that is ours?*

During our months of isolation, I became fanatical about writing in my journal, which I did faithfully every evening after crawling into bed. I recorded how many new cases of Covid-19 appeared in the United States and in Portland, and how many people died. I always included the date and the hour of my writing—I needed to impose some order onto my existence, because my days were all running into the same river. Just the telling of the (inconceivably boring) activities of each day was grounding for me. *I did the laundry, called my sister in Alabama, saw the Golden State Warriors beat Milwaukee.* Reminds me of the five-year diaries I kept as a child: *I rode bikes after school. We had fried chicken for dinner.* Otherwise, my experience was threatening to become ethereal. Sometimes I felt as though I existed in some kind of weird alternative universe, or maybe didn't exist at all.

The only two people I visited during the pandemic were Kelly and Peter. Kelly's my new best friend. She's a mostly retired research physician and an excellent seamstress, at a time when hardly anyone sews anymore. Last time we met, she was wearing a long blouse she created with a large likeness of John Brown on the front. Go figure. Her husband Peter is a medical researcher, too, a super-achiever who was still doing that work while also running a pig farm, providing meat for local restaurants when his life was turned upside down. Peter had a knee replacement and was doing amazingly well, climbing stairs he shouldn't be able to climb, when a freak accident happened: he fell and was paralyzed from the waist down. Doctors hoped to reverse the damage. They couldn't. I visited Kelly and Peter because I couldn't stand not to. My friend needed me. I love her and couldn't help her. I just showed up from time to time with food and wine and jokes—and a mask, of course. Since that time, through sheer will and determined exercise, Peter can walk with braces. Small miracles. I'll take it.

The numbers of the dead during the pandemic were abstract, but the scratching of my pencil was not, and so I recorded those ciphers, acknowledged the people they represented. I could not "adjust" to these unseemly deaths, hundreds of thousands of them, particularly the deaths of those considered unworthy of our concern: those frail of body and mind, trapped in nursing homes; those languishing in prisons, unvaccinated; the mentally ill, filling our streets. I numbered these journals on the front cover, one after the next after the next, an unending stream of living in the midst of dying. I have quite a nice black stack of them on my bookshelf. They are the journals of the plague years, insisting that we remember.

At the beginning of each journal is a statement placed there by the publisher: *If this journal is found, please return to owner*, followed by lines for my contact information. Next the publisher has printed the single word *Reward*, followed by a space, assuming that the owner of the journal would be so protective of the contents as to actually pay someone for returning it. These journals will be sent along with the rest of my papers to Meadville Lombard Seminary after my death. The fact is, I can't imagine anyone ever reading them.

Will my children peruse them after I'm gone? After my death, one of my sons—deep in grief, I presume—might see the stack, pick one up, and casually page through it. He'll find nothing literary, nothing clever. Just the stuff of living each day in isolation. He will stop shortly and toss it aside, saying to his brother, *I didn't know Mom had such an empty life.*

*I am in a bookstore, about to give a reading. No one is showing up. Three or four finally arrive. Another reader is scheduled to come after me, and someone asks for the other reader, says he'll return when it's time for her. The owner finally introduces me, begins by saying my book has been very popular, which I suspect is a lie. She says that Thomas Merton has endorsed it, which I know, of course, is a lie. He's dead. Am I dead, too?*

......

I started doing research on this book fourteen years ago, and halfway through that time, began writing the text. I struggled mightily with the organizational structure, creating an outline, then another, then another, then another, ad infinitum. Nothing worked.

But then the long-coveted vaccine came, and eventually the masks came off. I stopped being afraid to draw near, to touch. George and I went to our favorite restaurant—outside in the chilly air at first, still wary—and ordered grilled salmon on Caesar salad and a glass of pinot gris. One day I was moved to pick up my manuscript and go through it—was there anything of value here, or should I just toss it? I found I liked much of what I saw. All on its own, while I was away from it, the book had morphed into memoir. The time away had given me the perspective I needed, and the structure made itself known, effortlessly. I began writing again, and with such joy! *This book is going to happen!* But it has been a long, long time in coming.

# 41

# *What Goes, What Stays*

*She sorts through her winter clothes, hanging some of them securely in plastic zip-lined bags for storage. The sweaters are put in soft plastic square containers. Other garments go in the long blue polyester bag with a cord tie at the top, for a trip to the cleaners. She and George go to lunch at the Old Spaghetti Factory, where she orders "endless soup and salad," eats a bowl of minestrone soup, a salad with balsamic vinaigrette dressing and blue cheese crumbles, then a second. Endless is an attractive concept.*

*They drive across the river to the shop that's repairing George's glasses because the frames were not done properly the first time. The repair has not been finished—the glasses are promised in one hour. They race to the salon where Chelsea cuts her hair just the way she wants it cut. They wend their way back through the late-afternoon traffic to the eyeglass place, where they learn that the glasses cannot be repaired there but must be sent to the home office somewhere far, far away. They drive home in even worse traffic, finally arriving at their condo, and share a cool drink of tonic water and lime.*

*She begins cooking dinner, scrubbing the beets, washing the greens. She puts water on to boil for the shrimp and throws in the Cajun seasoning. They finish dinner, and she prepares coffee, decaf for her, caf for George, and slices a mango for dessert, squeezing lime juice over the slices and sprinkling them with a touch of nutmeg.*

*She and George have a conversation about the Golden State Warriors, the current obsession that takes their minds off national politics. Steph is greater than ever this year, will Draymond Green ever grow up? She takes the clothes out of the dryer, folds them, puts them away. She crawls into their big bed, reads for an hour or longer, until she can't keep her eyes open. If I die before I wake. Becoming unconscious in sleep is far too close to death for her—always, she fights sleep. She finally turns out the bedside light. She is awakened three or four times during the night, once to go to the bathroom, once because of George's snoring, once because of a disturbing dream. A day in her life, since retirement.*

......

Novelty is not of great interest to me these days. George and I get fancy brochures in the mail about exotic places—India, Antarctica, the Galapagos Islands. After three years, the pandemic is over, pretty much done with. *We could travel*, we say. And then we don't. Faraway places no longer call to us, for we feel, strangely, that we've already been everywhere. Penguins, tigers? We can watch them on TV, guided by the sonorous voice of David Attenborough. Now we take satisfaction in gathering our experiences, memories, dreams into patterns. Structures of meaning are revealing themselves, and we need time to absorb and reflect.

Increasingly, I understand that my possessions are constraining. I'm beset by all the stuff filling our space, much of which we don't use or want, but which we've passively allowed to accumulate. Gifts we don't need. Clothing we no longer wear. Kitchen devices that haven't been moved from their place in the pantry for years. We don't clear out our space often enough—we push forward with whatever project draws our interest. And then, of course, there's the ridiculous covetousness: *but I might need that someday.*

Consider clothing. I buy a few new pieces each season, but since I have left my professional life, I don't actually need more clothing. Why do I buy anything at all? As I flip through the pages of a favorite catalog, I drift to an imaginative place where my body is loose and free of pain, and I'm as elegant and unconstrained as the models seem to be. Newness of clothing is tantamount to newness of person, perhaps? *In that soft cashmere sweater, I would feel young, lithe, hopeful, ever expectant of invitations to laugh, to love.* It's the adult version of "playing dress-up"—nothing wrong with that, so long as I don't take it too seriously. So long as I remember that in my real world, cashmere scratches.

We have to care for, in some manner or other, each item we own. Richard Avedon's solution to his soul-sucking accumulation of possessions is instructive. At one point in his life, he emptied his home of everything—every stick of furniture, every painting, every dish, every book—then started over. He brought back into his living space only those items which were genuinely useful or brought him joy. Like Avedon, I want my life unencumbered with whatever is not life-giving. Or at least that's what I say to myself. I do keep our living space tidy—but deep clearing takes time, and time is at a premium, so "later," I say—just now, I'm greedy to create.

The current "tidying" craze, advocated by tidiness czar Marie Kondo (*The Life-Changing Magic of Tidying Up*) is too extreme for me. Kondo says that your past weighs you down, and so don't stow belongings—get rid of whatever items are not currently meaningful. But discernment is sometimes difficult. *What in the past is holding me, and what is holding me back?*

I can definitely do without the parrot alarm clock given to me by a friend whose surname is Polly—at the set time, the parrot keeps shrieking "Wake up! Wake up! Wake up!" I'll be glad to give away the too-small pajamas I bought on sale, without trying them on. I'm more than willing to sell most of my books, using the money for new books. There are, though, a couple of shelves of books that I will keep near me for as long as I live—Thomas Merton, James Hillman, Thich Nhat Hanh, Carl Jung, Susan Griffin, Wendell Berry, Dorothy Day, not to mention my grandmother's Bible. These writers have guided me along my perilous journey and have become friends I cherish and still consult.

And what about the tiny antique ceramic house gifted to me by an elderly friend in Liverpool, where I lived for a while as a young married woman? This gracious lady, who suffered terribly from arthritis, made a Christmas cake for my husband and me and perched the little house on top. I can still picture her dapper husband with the thin mustache, taking their corgi for a walk. I keep this little house on my meditation table to remind me of those who suffer in silence, with no remedy. And to remind myself that I, being human, will also suffer and so will not be surprised and alarmed when suffering comes. Or what about Lion, a stuffed animal my best friend, Melissa, gave me when

I needed courage? I was with Melissa when she died twenty-five years ago—hardly seems possible. Lion rests on my bed. Grrrrrrr! When I feel particularly bereft, weak of body and spirit, I can cuddle with Lion. These tangible objects connect me to my past, to people who act as a ballast against the uncertainties of life. *Ah, you were there, and you're still here, caught fast in memory.*

# 42

# *Living in Love*

I go to a movie, get a bag of popcorn, and enter a world of imagination, different from the one I encounter as I leave the theater. I blink my eyes, fumble for my sunglasses. I see Mandy, the homeless woman selling the newspaper *Street Roots*. She's always there, it's her claimed spot. "My picture's in this issue!" she says, and smiles as if she owns the world. She knows we're good for a couple of bucks, some gab. She has time. Now I have time.

I'm learning for the first time the power of gratitude. Yesterday I had an MRI. A strapping young technician came for me and said, "My name is Harun, and I'll be helping you today." I asked him where he was from, and as I had guessed, he said Bosnia. No time to find out more, what he had been through, when and why he had moved to Portland. He explained that the procedure would be short, gave me protection for my ears, lent his strong arm as I climbed unsteadily onto the table. Several times as the grating, knocking sounds assaulted me, I heard his reassuring voice from the microphone, "You're doing great." The test done, he placed my shoes back on and tied them. Waiting until my dizziness subsided, he then helped me to my feet. I said to him, "Nobody likes to have an MRI, but your kindness has made my experience so easy."

He smiled and said, "It doesn't cost me anything to be nice." Me either. Just noticing and mentioning.

Family has emerged as a greater focus since my retirement. My younger sister Donna and I have taken a couple of road trips together: a self-directed blues tour from Southern Alabama to Memphis, stopping at hole-in-the-wall juke joints along the way. In Clarksdale, Mississippi, we stumbled into

"Red's," a small, dark club with no sign out front, where we heard the amazing Watermelon Slim play his slide guitar, and drank Bud Light (cash only) with the rest of the customers. Most recently, we drove all along Southern Louisiana, listening to zydeco music at a festival and the next day driving to Avery Island, where the same family has been making Tabasco, our hot sauce of choice, for five generations. Donna and I have so very much in common—both English teachers, now both writers and social justice activists. Both of us are passionate and engaged, both vulnerable to slights, and both still feel the need to be heard, something that wasn't possible when we grew up.

When I was ministering, my energy went to my congregants, to my sermons, to civic engagement. I always kept in touch with my two sons, who live in Kentucky, but now I have more bandwidth to listen to their concerns or just connect with them and see what's happening in their lives. I'm curious about their opinions on everything from politics to movies. I have a grandson who has turned out to be a gifted saxophone player—where that came from, who knows? Now he's graduating from a conservatory and has just taken a much-coveted job with "Pershing's Own," the US Army Band. He lives far from me, but we FaceTime regularly and are drawing closer.

George has two daughters and four grandchildren in Portland, so we share many holidays and birthdays with his family. I follow with interest the vagaries in the lives of his daughters, both single moms at this point, both pushing hard with the demands of work and children.

George and I don't want to hoard our savings and then, as I said to George jokingly, "die and leave everything to our thankless children." I've noticed that I'm becoming more generous. Maybe that's because I've internalized more fully the fact of my own mortality. Money can protect us from some things but not from everything. Not loneliness. Not illness and death. The practice of "saving for the future" morphs into "what can I give?" How much, how soon?

I'm interested in creating pods of time with people we care about. George and I have financed family trips at Christmas so that members of different generations can be together. We've gathered his family and mine for a week in a small hotel in Mexico and another time, in a large Airbnb in New Orleans. George and I exchange visits every year with a couple we are close to in San

Francisco. On our last visit, we took them as our guests to a beach house on the Oregon coast for four very special days.

I'm watching myself forgive more readily. As a child, I always thought that one day some mysterious switch would click on, and *daddy would stop drinking, see the error of his ways, will love me the way I always wanted to be loved.* Even the most loving, the most faithful people betray us in little and not-so-little ways. Their behavior is generally not willful or meant to harm—it was built in years before we even came along. And in the end, they have the audacity to die. To be a grown-up is to learn not to take their behavior personally. We ourselves, in an absolute way, cannot be other than who we are, with our own particular history and predilections. With this understanding, we find it possible to forgive both ourselves and those dear to us, those who obstinately continue to be themselves instead of the people we want them to be, for our sake.

I am increasingly loath to give advice. Once I did a lot of that, especially to my grown children, my sister, sometimes to friends. It's not really helpful, and it's not welcome. When I venture there, I'm always sorry and afterward tell myself to *never do that again!* Nothing that I could say to caution or to guide could possibly be as valuable as my presence, my witness. I can pay close attention, listen well. I can smile. I can touch. I can find another worthy. I can bless.

*I'm encamped in the apartment of my grown son, who has just suffered heartbreak. He's forty-five and thought he was going to marry the only woman he has ever really loved. He's fine until he speaks of her, then he cannot control his tears.*

*He has just moved into a third-floor walk-up, and boxes are piled high in every corner. The fridge contains apples and beer. I've flown thousands of miles to be with him. I want to fix his pain. But I blunder into his grief, asking questions, giving advice.*

*The first morning arrives, cold and dreary. He has already left for work by the time I get up, groggy from jet lag. I stumble into the kitchen to make a cup of coffee, but there's no coffee. I rummage through a box of his books, looking for something to read. I find a book by James Carse and remember that I sent it* to my son when he was in college. I begin reading an essay, "A Shared Silence," and I note on page 159 my son has underlined the words "not until my mother was long dead," and has written in the tiniest of letters possible, in pencil, hardly legible, "I don't want my mother to die!" I wonder what fears, what longings triggered that notation, the only one throughout the article. I find a place of silence within.

Over the next few days, my son and I sample the town's restaurants, we eat fat sandwiches and coconut cream pie with mounds of meringue; we play country music and sing along with the lyrics, in full voice; we cheer as the Golden State Warriors soundly defeat the Pelicans; we go to a silly movie, and I laugh so loud that my son shushes me, embarrassed.

After three days, I fly back home. My seatmate wants to tell me about his important job with high tech, about this important trip to India he's on. I smile and turn away, close my eyes. My son's silence is all around me, a shared silence, holding us tighter than ever before.

．．．．．．

I'm thinking back to my fortieth birthday. I was in Berkeley, going to seminary at the time, and having just returned from a trip the previous evening, I hadn't arranged for any kind of celebration with friends. Loneliness washed over me. I decided to walk out my door without a destination and just see where I was led. I strolled through the tree-lined neighborhood and then walked down to the food ghetto where Chez Panisse reigns. Even lunch was too expensive there, so I went to my favorite Thai restaurant, then the coffee shop across the street, for a decaf cappuccino and a pastry filled with custard. All the heaven I needed.

That day has become a template for the way I want to live—as I age, I'm not fraught with the pressures of destination: I have only this day, this hour, this moment. Better to live with presence, rather than in some imaginary future. Of course, there are always tasks that we'd rather not do, but even these, we can do mindfully. As Thich Nhat Hanh teaches, "Wash the dishes just to wash the dishes." I'm beginning to see the depth and pleasure of an encounter as the true measure of joy, rather than the unrelenting cataloging of accomplishment. Still hard for me, though, after a lifetime of *doing*.

When I'm not so task-oriented, so given to the demands of the ego, I'm surprised by the opportunities that light on my plate. Just by being available, I come upon people who need a kind word or a bit of encouragement. In my past oh-so-busy life, I would have roared past them, on my way to the current project capturing my attention. I'm realizing that it's these frothy exchanges that are the genesis of relationship. Opportunities arise for easy human interaction in the condo elevators, for example, and I find myself saying things like "Been grocery shopping, I see;" or even making one of the ubiquitous comments on the weather: "Nice to see the sun out"; or since many of the residents have dogs, I can always greet dog owners with, "What a cute dog!" And then the follow-up: "What's your dog's name?" Always a winner.

*I'm looking down the river walkway from my condo, three stories up. The scene is ordinary and at the same time extraordinary. There is an old man walking beside an old woman, presumably his wife, in a wheelchair being pushed by a young man, all in white. The husband is all in black: a black jacket, a billed cap, black. He slows his pace to match that of his wife. He reaches down and takes her hand, which seems inert; she keeps staring straight ahead, seemingly unaffected by his touch, as they continue along the walkway, both separate and together. On a parallel path, going in the opposite direction, a group of young people, all dressed in black—black clothing, black helmets—fly by on their bikes. As I study the scene, I begin to see myself at one with them, at one with the failing wife; the patient, loving husband; the young attendant; the bike club whizzing past. The watcher and the watched become undivided.*

# 43

# *Choosing Mercy over Judgment*

When I left my pulpit, my position of influence, I was forced to question the very concept of power and the pride that often accompanies it. It's easy for ministers to get an inflated ego, to speak *ex cathedra*. I was especially vulnerable because of my lifelong struggle to think of myself as honorable and worthy. Even in my relatively God-free, irreverent denomination, ministers are a stand-in for the Holy. We show up at the most significant moments in people's lives (marriage, illness, loss, death). We stand in a pulpit, wear robes, and speak to people about the deepest concerns of their lives. The temptation is to buy into the PR, even embellish it a bit. *Maybe I'm not perfect, but really close. Virtuous. And certainly entitled.* I was the senior minister of arguably the largest Unitarian Universalist congregation in the nation at that time, and I kept up with the membership stats to prove that to myself and, of course, to my peers that I was OK—not just OK, but superior, really the best. *My steeple is bigger than your steeple.* Staying in the numbers game, I've learned, always cheats the player.

······

Years ago, a question was posed to me by a half-drunk man at a small dinner party. "Do you have any regrets?" "No, not really," I answered. He became angry, verbally abusive, as he tried to force me to admit to something, *anything*. No dice. Actually, I was beginning to regret having come to this dinner party.

Now, though, I am ever more in touch with the dark side of my personality. I wake in the night. I have troubling dreams which give me hints about a reality that my consciousness has been bent on escaping.

I find myself falling into regret. *What? Am I not the good (really excellent!) person I always thought I was? Maybe not lovable, but always moral, always following the rules that good people follow. Work hard. Pursue excellence. Never, never tell a lie. Pay your debts. Vote in every election.* You get the picture. When I've been tempted to decry past behavior, my ego has generally come to the rescue. "I've always done my best," I would say to myself. "If I fell short, well, it was the best I could do at the time." Maybe, maybe not. What had seemed to be a closely woven fabric, clean and tight, began showing signs of weakness—threads were unraveling, even holes appearing. Now I would answer the dinner party guest differently.

*Your neglect, your missteps, your sins rise up. The self-respect that you worked for all your life—it came from the false picture, the paint-by-numbers that you showed to the world. Ah, now it's a messy image, with no clear form, all interlocking pieces, colors, shapes. You have joined the others, all those broken, deceived, cowardly, selfish, longing people who are . . . well, human. Welcome them. Welcome you.*

A practice I've had to reconsider: *tell the truth, above all, tell the truth.* I am remembering being at the bedside of Daisy Bingham, the former church secretary, a self-effacing older woman who had been faithful to the church over long years. Her home was a kind of dark hovel on the side of a busy road, the end result of marrying a dreamer who gave her five children but little else. Daisy is dying. A room in the church had long been called Bingham Hall, after her—the name evolved casually, but the church is now in full rehab mode, so Daisy asks me, "Will the church keep the name Bingham Hall?"

I say (the truth, of course), "I don't know." I've wondered more than once what I should have said. If I had the encounter to do over, I would have smiled, taken her hand, and said, "I expect so." Then I might have repeated, to reassure her, "Yes, I expect so." In fact, the name Bingham Hall has been retained. But she never knew.

Over the years, I've actually been fine with disregarding tact, imagining my blunt speech as truth writ large, an ethical plus. I've been one of those people who, if you ask me "Do I look fat in this dress?" will no doubt say "yes." I've been critical more often than kind. I've spoken too many times when I should have listened. I've insisted that I was "right" when right didn't matter, the person did.

Taking responsibility is one thing—on the other hand, falling into shame, wallowing in self-recrimination is not helpful. Having been raised a Catholic, then Southern Baptist, I was ripe for my lifelong addiction to guilt. Of course, I'm not the only one in our culture who has been seduced by the purity ethic. Augustinian self-loathing has deeply marked Christian culture. The earliest settlers in this country were far-left Puritans. Hardcore. Scratch a Puritan and you find a Calvinist, unredeemed and unredeemable. Not healthy. Not helpful.

I have a friend, Barbara, who was formerly the executive director of Greenpeace—she's highly intelligent and opinionated to the max. Once she said of herself, "I'm a difficult person," spoken as fact, not as judgment. I admired that casual acceptance of self. It's possible to acknowledge frailties, failures, without trying to make excuses, yet continue to deepen kindness and compassion, both for ourselves and for others. In fact, one doesn't happen without the other. It's a blessing to feel a bit freer of self: I have less to lose each day.

My Victorian grandfather, Big Papa, used to say grace at every meal. He would end with something like "May we walk circumspectly with thee." But once in a while, especially on holidays, he would call on my errant father, whom Papa characterized as "the black sheep" of his seven grown children. OK, fair enough—my father was an alcoholic who got in fights, ran with reprobates, gambled, and went to "roadhouses" on his way home from the oil rig. Not to mention the extensive number of girlfriends and the five wives. When Daddy had to pray, he always bowed his head, veiled his eyes with one calloused hand, and paused for a long time before he spoke, leaving us wondering if he was going to come through with a blessing, after all. Finally, he would pray, every time the same prayer: "Dear God, forgive me for all the dirty rotten things I've done." Then he would weep soft tears.

Even as a child who desperately wanted her father to stop drinking, I was pretty sure that God preferred Daddy's prayer. We're not asked to be perfect, we're asked to be faithful, to return again and again after violating the values we claim, the good we would do. Our failings serve us well—as we flail around in the muddy flats of life, they push us helplessly to God.

Sometimes transformation does occur, coming as a benevolent thief in the night, taking away some hardness or some sadness I thought would always be a part of me, allowing me to forgive another, or myself, or perhaps shifting my values, as I increasingly choose mercy over judgment. We can't force these changes, we can merely allow them.

*I'm wandering in a used furniture store, just hanging out with my best friend Melissa, who is to die far too soon, only a few months later from the cancer she has endured for two years. The owner has for sale not only furniture but paintings, ceramic figures, rugs, mirrors, and other such items. Way in the back of the shop, in the midst of these cluttered offerings, I spy her sitting alone—Quan Yin, the Chinese bodhisattva, the Goddess of Compassion, the "one who hears the cries of the world." I go for a closer look, am fixated by the peace she radiates. I know I have to have her, but such beauty will be costly. "How much?" I ask the shopkeeper.*

*"Fifty dollars," he says. "She has two broken fingers." I look closely and see the little finger and ring finger of one hand are broken off. Melissa insists on buying her for me as a gift, a parting gift, I sense. That was twenty-five years ago, and my Quan Yin still sits in the middle of my meditation table, calling me to quiet each day, to compassion, and to mercy. Reminding me of Melissa, who loved me like I was her own child. Broken as I was, broken as I am.*

# 44

# *The Scream of a Whistle*

Because my schedule is no longer determined by the needs of an institution, I sometimes find myself floating free, detached. Bored, as it were, with living, especially when I've finished a writing project. Postpartum depression, I think. Depression has been after me all my adult life, and I accept as inevitable its coming and going. *No fucking big deal.* But these days, I sense another layer, a new vulnerability. I wonder if this post-retirement ennui is simply "keeping the lid on," as my old Gestalt teacher Neil Lamper would say. In my case, keeping the lid on the darkness to come.

*I reach in the fridge and grab one of the tiny tins of tomato juice I keep there—my thirty-calorie snack. I'm not hungry for food anyway. But I am hungry. I drain the can down to the very last drop, and as I finish, I think of death, draining the life all the way down until there is nothing left, just the empty container, no more red stuff inside.*

Though this is not the way I want to live, it's still hard for me to stop grabbing and crashing, stumbling through my days. *Running, running, running.* Reading the (two) papers; emptying the dishwasher, filling it again; checking/answering email; phone calls/Zoom calls; making medical appointments/canceling appointments; going to medical/dental appointments; doing the laundry, folding clothes; checking out catalogs I like, to see if there's anything, anything at all that I want; ordering stuff online; returning stuff I ordered and don't want; doing exercises for my ankle and hip; checking out new recipes; making a grocery list; running to the grocery store, stopping by the pet shop for shrimp/chicken wet food my cat will eat, stopping by the drug store for some more Tylenol; watching David Attenborough and various fetching animals hunt or be hunted, on TV; cheering for the Golden State Warriors and watching Steph play; scanning miscellaneous books, articles, whatever draws my attention. *Don't stop, don't stop, never stop!* Distracting myself, keeping me occupied lest I drop a stitch and find the abyss opening below.

*Something is after her! She senses this encroaching danger creeping in most acutely at sunset, the final scene of the day, when a blue, blue stain begins creeping in. At the end of the film or the meal or the book, a strange emptiness enters, and she considers what she can do to fill the void. Anything will do. Anything. "How about a cup of tea?" she says to her husband.*

*She's a runaway train hurtling down the track, like in those old cowboy movies—out of control, sure to go off the rails, never to reach its destination. Oh, but there's no destination in this movie—just the villain Time and a train rushing nowhere.*

······

Every now and then a feeling of sheer despair rolls through me. *What's causing this attack of angst?* The years sneak up on you like a stranger in a B-rated horror movie, and all of a sudden, time is short. The sun slips behind the horizon, darkness falls, opaque and heavy, whatever good that has been done is put to rest, silence gathers in the gloom. I think I'm grieving in anticipation of the loss of light, the dark that envelops everything in the end.

*Robins nested in a small tree outside my kitchen window for years—each spring they returned, producing tiny fledglings with fragile wings and open bills; every year I watched the babies grow and finally fly. That is, until this year. Dark avengers in the shape of crows came and attacked the nest, stabbing the hatchlings with their long black beaks. The crows didn't want to eat, just wanted to kill. Hearing the parent birds' mournful cries, and going to investigate, I found the tiny broken bodies inert on the ground. For several hours the robins circled round their dead, calling, grieving, helplessly protesting the loss of their little ones. This was life insisting upon life, their fierce judgment against death.*

Each of us one day will be gone. How can I not *be*? *Impossible*. Once I was *not*, then I *was*, and now I *am*. Am I not *something*? Do I not have a soul, or am I nothing more than a bag of chemicals? How can the *me* that I have so treasured and cared for, not exist? The me that worked so relentlessly on perfecting myself. Self as a social construct? Hardly comforting.

As I write, Ian McKellen, eighty-two years of age and widely regarded as one of the finest actors of stage and screen, is currently doing *Hamlet* at the Theater Royal in Windsor, England. In a moving documentary, *McKellen: Playing the Part*, McKellen reflects on his life and career. At one point he says, "Why doesn't anyone tell you that when you get old, you think about death all the time?"

*I'm out shopping for shoes, Melissa says she wants to go with me—she knows death is creeping up on her, we use any excuse to be together. I try on several pairs of shoes, choose one, and I think we're done. But Melissa says maybe she'll look for shoes, too. The clerk brings out a handsome pair of mahogany walking shoes, unlaces one, and she slips it on. It fits her slender foot precisely. "These shoes will last you twenty years!" he says with the confidence of the young, as he reaches for the mate. "Maybe not today," Melissa says.*

It is occurring to me, rather late on, I regret to say, that self-development might not be the sine qua non of existence. For me, too, the time will come for the last pair of good shoes. The last trip abroad. I'll probably never make it to Greece or to the Taj Mahal or to the Galapagos Islands to see the giant tortoises. I'm already driving what will most likely be my last car. It's too late to get a puppy, a friend says of herself—*you don't want to die before your dog, right?* I'm going to leave this good earth with tasks uncompleted, with letters unanswered, with books unread (I've always known I would read Proust someday), and with books unwritten. No doubt I will die without being forgiven by some, without my forgiving others, in spite of my resolution to do so.

*Hold back nothing, Marilyn, nothing: money or breath or love, because one day your ability to touch another, to kiss, to heal, to forgive will be no more.*

Because my primary, my *primal* commitment is to the Spirit, I am pulled back repeatedly to question my motives, my behavior, and to search out what

I'm currently supposed to be doing with my time and energy, both of which appear to be waning at a disturbing rate. I think of Flannery O'Connor and the lupus that allowed her to write only a few hours a day. I think of Tom Lubbock, the art critic whose brain was riddled with cancer. He continued to write, struggling to find words, up until the final few days of his life. I tell myself, OK, get on with it and quit the complaining, ditch the excuses.

......

*I am at the bedside of Marcia, a former congregant and sister minister, who is dying. I am holding her hand, which has grown somehow incredibly small, now like the hand of a child, the nails transparent, perfect. Restless, she clasps my hand with an uncharacteristic urgency. In the end state of mesothelioma, she can hardly speak for want of breath. She says, "I'm confused about what's happening next." I tell her she is held in love. She says, "I want to believe in life." Is Marcia telling me she is not ready to die? I lean over her, place my hand round the side of her head, whisper a prayer of peace for her. I'm torn—I can't stay with her—other promises pull me out of the hospice room, out where George is waiting in the car. I take my hand from hers, though she is still holding on tightly. I go on with my life, as she is leaving hers.*

I thought about Marcia's words for weeks, for months. *I want to trust life.* More than anyone I know, she did just that. As I recall that evening, now two years later, I think her words were a confirmation of the way she lived—and died. They were the words of Thomas, impugned as "doubting Thomas": "I believe," he said to Jesus. "Help thou my unbelief." I love this story—Thomas's honesty, his struggle, his absolute refusal to deny his very human need to know the truth, beyond a doubt.

I think of Jesus's torment in the Garden of Gethsemane: "If it be thy will, let this cup pass from me." Jesus knew, had known for some time, what life would demand of him. He understood and accepted his destiny. But in his humanity, he had to question: *Is this death on the cross what is demanded of me—really?* Later, as Jesus is hanging in agony upon the cross, dying there in disgrace, his apostles having fled, with a thief on either side, he calls out, "My God, my God, why have you forsaken me?"

Is not this the natural, almost predictable question of each of us as we die, as we lose everything—not just everything we love, as some people say, but as we lose the only existence we have known, as we lose consciousness itself, the very capacity that has allowed us to choose faith? *Have I been forsaken?*

*Last night, still in a dream state, I twice hear the scream of a train whistle cutting through the dark. What a mournful cry! Going nowhere, nowhere, nowhere, with its big eye on the track, in such a rush, such anguish.*

The child emerges from the womb—leaving everything that is safety, security, warmth—leaving home. There is the shock of light, of air on limbs, of strange hands on flesh, pulling the child into an existence that is uncertain, one that will remain uncertain, all through life. So the baby cries—not just cries, but as I remember the birthing of my sons—*shrieks*. All has been lost! The baby has no promise of anything whatsoever, the brain being just a simple searching machine at this point. Then comes the mother's arms, her breast. And forevermore exists the search for the Absolute Wholeness that was found in the womb. Is that to be found only in death? Only when everything we've ever known is gone? Do we then return to the Wholeness from which we came?

・・・・・・

Of late, I have a new spiritual practice. My therapist—who is not just an excellent counselor but also a writer of spiritual matters—has suggested just stopping from time to time and taking "a sacred pause": turning off the racing mind, taking a few deep breaths, allowing my body to relax. Commonly, I go out on the deck and check on my geraniums, which are exceptionally beautiful this year. I soak the plants, give them a refreshing spray of water on their leaves. I chuck them under the chin for good measure. Or I just watch the changing face of the river as it slips quietly by our condo. Or I take my kitten, Bella, into my arms like the baby she is and tell her she is a good cat.

A few days ago I was taking one of these pauses, watching the light on the river. The time is early evening, not quite dusk. The river is still, the surface shimmering with a delicate salmon color, a reflection from the setting sun. On the other side of the river is an island, a heron rookery, its rich green growth darkening as night approaches. The herons, gigantic birds that soar through the sky during the day like lazy pterodactyls, are snuggled down in their nests with their young. The clouds are flushed with a numinous light, the same exquisite color rippling over the water.

All at once, I am struck by a singular thought: *I'm not afraid to die.*

I'm not persuaded that this understanding is more than momentary. Will I take this assurance with me through the years ahead, however many or few they may be? When I understand that my death is imminent, will I be at peace with that? I don't know. But I do know that at that moment, on that evening, all was well with my soul. I didn't want anything to be other than precisely what it was, and my warrior impulse had been put to bed. Since then I've been calmer, more settled in mind and spirit. Easier to be around. More accepting of pain, of people . . . more accepting of what *is*.

I had an MRI recently and, whoops, they found a lesion that they weren't looking for on one of my ovaries. It happens. *It's probably benign*, my doctor said. *But we need to do some more imaging.* Turns out that I'm OK, *surely a relative term*, but I was led to contemplate the worst, a useful exercise. The worst that can happen is that I will die. Which is what everyone does. Which is what every living thing does. When you understand that, says Sallie Tisdale in her wise book *Advice for Future Corpses*, death ceases being a problem—it's simply the way things are. Steely logic there. Quite honestly, it's not the dying but the living well that's hard. Trying not to betray anyone . . . including and most prominently, myself. Carrying the pain, carrying the loss. Not letting the last of life take you out of life.

# 45

# *Nothing, No Matter How Precious, Can Be Kept*

George went in for a routine check-up, and his doctor detected a mass in his prostate. She was . . . concerned. Tests followed, then the diagnosis: George has prostate cancer that had already metastasized to four places in his bones.

First, there's the shock—*how can this be, when George seems so healthy, when he's a man who's hardly ever been to a doctor, who takes no medications whatsoever, at the age of seventy-nine?* Then we looked at the stats. According to the mortality rates for this diagnosis, *it appears that . . . it seems that . . . it is likely that . . . .* he will be dead in two years. Only 27 percent of men make it past five years.

Fear registered in me like a warning light, on and off, on and off: *George, no George, George, no George.* Of course, nobody really knows when a given individual will die. The oncologist himself said that he's had patients with this same diagnosis live ten years or more. He didn't say how many. We didn't ask. He also said, "We can keep you comfortable at the end." Not really a good idea to add that.

. . . . . .

I'm writing on my laptop here by the fireplace, my back supported, in my lookalike Eames chair from IKEA. No need for a fire today, though—we're expecting the temperature to go to 106 degrees, tomorrow to 116. A "heat dome," they're calling it. The wildfires have already started, way before summer.

I glance to my left and see George in his white waffle-weave bathrobe, identical to mine. We're a pair. He has fallen asleep in his easy chair, even though it's 9:40 a.m. Since his cancer diagnosis and the drug regimen he's on, he has been fatigued, takes lots of naps. The sun is streaming through the tall glass window of the condo, the brightness falling on the top of his downturned head, flowing over his body, his legs crossed. When he's so terribly still this way, I think maybe he's dead. I look carefully and see that his chest is rising and falling. I release my breath.

George is polite in that fashion of well-brought-up men of his generation. Although I'm quite capable of opening doors, he unfailingly opens them for me. I dare not say *I've misplaced my glasses* because he will stop whatever he is doing and find them for me. He puts a fresh glass of water at my bedside each night. His attentiveness to me clearly gives him pleasure, and my part is to accept his caring gestures. Was it by accident that I have chosen such a partner? I think not—I've never left behind my yearning to be cared for.

*I'm in our walk-in closet where I've sought refuge from my troubled mind by ironing George's white handkerchiefs. I got them from Helmer's, the best men's store in town. George has quite a stash that I replenish when they get the least bit ragged. I spray eight of the white squares with water, place each on top of the last, then iron them one by one. My hot iron glides over the surface. I fold the handkerchief in half, press the iron again into the fabric, fold again, iron again, until I have a perfect little white square, just right for his pocket. Classy! Like George.*

I know that it's likely I'll be alone again one day. I can hardly imagine it, so rich my life has become. *What if we had married fifty years ago, when we were both young?* It's a fantasy with yearning but no wings: all that he has been, all that he is, has been delivered to me in a silver cup. I drink daily from it.

One evening, George knocked over a little ceramic vase I got from a primitive kiln in Guatemala, and it broke beyond repair. I said, "That vase came from South America." An unnecessary and unkind comment which I immediately regretted. I left the room and a few minutes later heard George weeping as he was picking up the broken pieces. He said, "I don't know why I'm crying," but he couldn't stop. He has such a tender heart these days. I took him in my arms, tried to comfort him. Nothing, no matter how precious, can be kept.

I don't believe George will die, ever. I can't wrap my head around that thought. My plan is that we'll both stay healthy and live until he's 104 and I'm 100, then we'll both die more or less at the same time of something quite painless. Not suddenly, like a fatal heart attack or a car accident—no, something that gives us time to say goodbye in some graceful fashion, but doesn't make us in any drastic sense uncomfortable. In case things don't work out quite this way, though, we're getting our wills in order.

George says he hopes I die before he does, because after all who would take care of me? If George does die first, then my mettle will be tested as never before. He's been there for fifteen years to counter my anxiety, my loneliness. He still goes to his office one day a week. When he leaves, he kisses me and says, "I'll miss you!" and he actually means it. I laugh it off, tease him, and say, "I'll miss you *so much*! Get out of here."

Although George is now often fatigued and susceptible to depression, he is doing exceptionally well—he's currently seven years post-diagnosis. Several years ago, he published *Fixing Your City*, a well-received book on new urban design, focusing on the climate crisis. A pilot program based on the book has been endorsed both by the mayor of Portland and also by Bill McKibben.

Why is it that when I say my prayers of gratitude and petition, my heart fills with lovingkindness for friends who are suffering, but when I try to pray for George, my prayers just stick in my throat: *don't do this to me*! I'm moving into strange territory, like in *Grimms' Fairy Tales*, where a walk in the woods means being surprised by fearsome creatures at every turn. Will there be room for hope or joy when George dies?

Having wrestled my whole life with my demons of self-doubt, I have read spiritual classics, oh so many (the *Bible* as a constant, of course, then everything from Augustine to Thomas Merton to Alan Watts, to Dorothy Day, to Eckhart Tolle, to the Dalai Lama, etc., etc.); I've read much of the great literature of the world; I've had wise teachers; many therapists; several spiritual directors; friends who will never let me go—and yet I could never completely shake the sense that I'm somehow not lovable, just flawed in the making, *dear God, how could you?* That is, until George showed up, insisting that he loved me, in spite of my internal protestations: *how could this wise and beautiful man make such a mistake?* I finally had to take him at his (repeated, insistent) word.

For the past fifteen years, I have had a partner who knows me as no other person has ever known me: my insecurities have been laid out before him, my unkindness, my leaning into judgment—and yet he has an inexplicable, inordinate love for me. The question of my worth still gnaws at me in weak and troubled moments, of course, but the evidence is striking and will take me beyond his death: *because of his preposterous love, I can never again doubt that I am lovable.* This is what is known as an act of grace. It simply lights on your plate, and you can do nothing beyond accepting it, with awe and abiding gratitude. Drink fully, drain the glass.

# 46

# The Order of Things

I wake, but I'm not fully conscious. Words arise from an interview I heard last evening with the great Swedish director Ingmar Bergman. The interviewer asks, "Why did you write *The Seventh Seal*?"—Bergman's signature film in which a medieval knight plays a game of chess with Death, who has come for him. Bergman says that he used to think about death constantly, and he wrote *The Seventh Seal* to consider death directly. After he completed that film, he says, he still thought about death, but the obsessing was gone.

Why did I remember these words, when so much of the rest of yesterday was relegated to the vague and inconsequential past? I am inundated with information. And I am choked to sickness with entertainment. During the night, my brain sorted through the dreck, dove deep, found the essential. I need to assimilate my experiences, to tie the present to the past, to see the themes that have driven me, to move in wise and more gentle ways in the final portion of my life. First we *grow*; then we *do*; and finally we *discover*. The path of life and death, a biological imperative for all living creatures, has a different dimension for us human creatures: we're the only ones called to make sense of it. Bergman had to make sense of it. And I do, too.

The film *All Is Lost*, starring Robert Redford, is an iconic treatment of our search for meaning. Redford portrays a sailor caught at sea, alone, in a sinking boat. He is a man of good sense, physical strength, and great resourcefulness. He does not talk—he considers, he decides, he acts, fully present to the moment. We see him patching the hole in his boat, righting his overturned life raft, learning how to navigate by sextant and sun.

But like us, The Man—he is not named, so I will call him The Man—is vulnerable to forces beyond his understanding and control. He is injured, he runs out of water, he becomes totally exhausted. His raft bobs about helplessly, a dot on the endless sea. The Man does everything right. He repairs the hole in his damaged craft, he climbs the mast to restore power to his radio, he even figures out how to desalinate seawater. He sends up flares to attract passing cargo ships—he yells out, "I'm here! I'm here." It is the plaintive cry of each human being to the universe, "I exist!" However, as Stephen Crane put it, the universe replies, "That fact has not created in me a sense of obligation." The ships pass by, ignoring The Man.

When the end seems inescapable, The Man stops his anxious striving. He writes a letter of regret and apology—he sums up his life, saying he tried to be strong and loving and right, but admits that he didn't always live up to his values. We do not know The Man's specific failures and regrets—his letter is directed to no spouse or child or friend.

He seems to be a decent man of strong character, a trustworthy man. But like all of us, he has had his blunders and betrayals. We do know that he wishes he had been more faithful to these unnamed others, and he wants them to know that he has done his best. He closes his letter, "I fought to the end. I'm not sure what that's worth. But I know that I did." In a gesture of futility, he seals the letter in a jar and drops the jar into the vast, indifferent sea. He understands that the chances of anyone's finding his letter are next to nil, but he must try to say goodbye, to explain his life and his choices to those he loves.

The end of the film is both highly suggestive and yet inconclusive. As The Man surrenders his life to the sea, he is not thrashing about like one who is drowning—he simply sinks slowly under the waves. Then he sees a light above him and swims eagerly toward it. A hand reaches down from the light, and the screen goes dark. Is The Man literally being saved, as all the audience members are hoping? Or is he having a pathetic last fantasy that he will be rescued? Is he having a near-death experience, which has been described by many as a journey to the Light? Or is he dying, with the Light guiding his way to the ultimate source of Love? The viewer must decide.

At the end of life, what has true significance? What we have achieved, who we have triumphed over, fades in importance. What gives meaning to our days is precisely Our Man's fervent desire to be true, to be kind, to love. We know—all of us—that we have failed to some degree, we have missed the mark. But we want those we leave behind to know we did our best.

・・・・・・

The grief of loss, the debt of sadness must be paid. If your work has been the love of your life, it's hard to imagine ever being so enamored again. Or if you're partnered with someone who's so beautifully right for you, how are you to face being alone?

When I consider the future, I am reduced, once again, to raw faith. No certainties, only surrender. If I can yield, new openings will come. Yes, at any age. Up until and including the last day of my life. My joints creak, my flesh aches, the dream shifts—one stream has gone dry, but another beckons. *Through many dangers, toils, and snares, I have already come.*

I carry these thoughts from the bedroom into the large open space that serves as the living/dining area of our condo, and am soon caught by the vision of the Willamette River and Ross Island, which lies just across the water. The island, once mined for gravel, is now a wildlife sanctuary. It's early January, and a delicate peach light from the rising sun has turned the wintry trees into a tableau of black skeletal figures. The beauty captures me, holds my gaze. Two Canadian geese part the sky, heading south. Late in the year for them, I think—they've been caught by the coldest day yet on record this year. I see nine blue heron nests, black masses that grow bigger each year, now clearly visible in the nakedness of the trees, silently waiting in anticipation of the mating rituals of spring: the preening, the circular flights, the moaning calls. Later the chicks will hatch, turn up their skinny necks and yellow beaks, and cry for the food their parents will bring. And so, in due time, life returns. It always does. It's the order of things.

# *About the Author*

**Marilyn Sewell**, a retired minister, is known for her dynamic speaking and teaching, and her justice work. She is the author and editor of twelve books and many articles and essays. Her life journey is beautifully rendered in the award-winning documentary film, *Raw Faith*, based on her memoir. After careers as an English teacher, a clinical social worker, and a TV on-the-air personality giving advice—not to mention single mom—she went to seminary and brought her work experience together as the Senior Minister of the First Unitarian Church of Portland Oregon. There she served with distinction for seventeen years, during which time the church grew to be one of the largest UU churches in the nation. Marilyn retired in 2009, was named Minister Emerita, and a social justice lecture was established in her honor.

Marilyn is the editor of two celebrated collections of women's poetry, the award-winning *Cries of the Spirit* (1991) and *Claiming the Spirit Within* (*Beacon* 1996), as well as *Resurrecting Grace: Remembering Catholic Childhoods* (2001), *Breaking Free: Women of Spirit at Midlife and Beyond* (2004), and *In Time's Shadow: Stories About Impermenance* (2019). She lives in a condo along the beautiful Willamette River in Portland, OR, with her architect husband, George Crandall, and her cat, Bella. A lover of words, she spends most of her time reading and writing.